THE STRATEGY OF
POLITICAL REVOLUTION

MOSTAFA REJAI received his Ph.D. from the University of California at Los Angeles and is now professor of political science at Miami University (Ohio), where he has been the recipient of an outstanding-teaching award. He is the author of *Leaders of Revolution* (forthcoming) and editor of and contributor to *Decline of Ideology?* (1971) and *Democracy: The Contemporary Theories* (1967). He has coauthored *Ideologies and Modern Politics* (1971) and edited *Mao Tse-tung on Revolution and War* (1969, 1970). He has contributed to *The New Communisms* (1969) and *Dictionary of the History of Ideas* (forthcoming). His articles have appeared in *Comparative Political Studies, Ethics, Il Politico, International Philosophical Quarterly, International Studies Quarterly, Journal of Asian and African Studies, Orbis,* and other journals.

THE STRATEGY OF
POLITICAL REVOLUTION

Mostafa Rejai

Anchor Press

DOUBLEDAY & COMPANY, INC.

Garden City, New York

1973

The Anchor Press edition is the first publication of
THE STRATEGY OF POLITICAL REVOLUTION

Anchor Press edition: 1973

ISBN: 0-385-00268-8
Library of Congress Catalog Card Number 70–182918

PREFACE

This volume focuses attention on strategy in political revolution—"strategy" provisionally defined as the over-all plan for the deployment of human and material resources necessary for mounting revolutionary upheavals. Although the literature on political revolution is literally staggering, only scant attention has been devoted to the topic of strategy. Most writers on revolution have dealt with strategy only implicitly; a few others have discussed strategy explicitly, but almost exclusively in the context of Communist revolutions.[1] The absence of a general treatment of strategy as an entity in its own right is rather surprising, since strategy is the most significant component of political revolutionary movements, determining their failure or success.

The strategy of political revolution will be analyzed on a theoretical as well as an empirical plane. The theoretical discussion takes place in the three chapters of Part I. Chapter 1 develops what I hope is a fairly precise definition of political revolution. Chapter 2 constructs a typology of political revolution consistent with the definition developed in Chapter 1. Chapter 3 sets forth the theoretical components of strategy.

Much of the theoretical discussion is necessarily critical, but I hope not unfairly so. For reasons to be elaborated in Chapters 1 and 2, much work on political revolution has proceeded on questionable conceptual grounds. A major difficulty in approaching the literature on revolution is the imprecision with which key theoretical tasks have been performed. Note, for example, the many competing definitions of political revolution—a situation that, although not uncommon in the social sciences, is nevertheless increasingly untenable as we strive toward a more scientific status. Note also the conflicting typologies of political revolution, typologies in which even "riot," "rebellion," and "coup d'état" are treated as forms of political revolution. The conceptual synthesis attempted in Part I—a second objective of this book—points a way, I hope, toward a more adequate theoretical grounding of political revolution.

The empirical analysis of strategy is made in Part II, where the theory of strategy developed in Chapter 3 is applied to three political revolutions selected in the context of the typology of Chapter 2. The political revolutions in question—the Bolivian Revolution of 1952, the Vietminh Revolution of 1946–54, and the French Revolution of 1968—have been chosen in the light of certain criteria. All three revolutions took place in the postwar period. Of the three, one occurred in Latin America, one in Asia, and one in Europe. One exploded in an advanced industrial setting, one in a relatively backward but comparatively urban society, and one in a backward rural country.

The selection of France may raise an initial question in the reader's mind, but, as we shall see, the French upheaval of 1968 fully meets the criteria of political revolution set forth in Chapter 1. Equally significantly, the case of France confronts us with key questions of political revolution in advanced industrial societies.

In approaching the material in Part II, it must be stressed that I am not as interested in the history of individual political revolutions as in their analytical and empirical significance for the theory of strategy. Indeed, the empirical chapters may be inadequate as political histories, since they treat selectively only those topics considered relevant to the concept of strategy.

The concluding chapter pulls together the two major parts of the book. It does so by scrutinizing the concept of strategy in the light of data from the Bolivian, Vietminh, and French revolutions. And it concludes by considering the prospects for political revolution in advanced industrial societies, with particular reference to the United States. This relating of theory to empirical investigation (with respect to strategy) is a third objective of this volume.

Throughout the book, an attempt has been made to conduct the analysis on as objective a level as humanly possible. I am not concerned with passing moral judgment on political revolution—whether it is good or evil, whether it should be praised or condemned. Partly for this reason, I make no effort to evaluate the three political revolutions in terms of their accomplishments or shortcomings. Moreover, any attempt to do more than end the coverage of each revolution with its success or failure would take us beyond the realm of strategy. The central objective of this book, then, is simply to understand political revolution with special reference to strategy.

The book as a whole is the product of a long-standing interest—as well as the teaching of courses—in political revolution. I would like to thank the members of my political revolution seminar, with whom many of the conceptual problems raised in this book were initially discussed. For important research assistance in connection with the material in Part II, I am indebted to James A. Davis, William J. Nealon, Richard T. Saeger, and Robert A. Schumacher. I am grateful to Candace C. Conrad for helpful comments on the Bolivia chapter and for translation of Spanish material. I wish to thank William R. Campbell, Ted Robert Gurr, Warren L. Mason, and David Spitz for reading the manuscript in whole or in part and offering many provocative criticisms. My particular gratitude goes to Professor Gurr, whose thorough and meticulous reading of the manuscript contributed markedly to whatever merit the study might have. I am grateful to the Committee on Faculty Research, Miami University, for a summer research fellowship and other assistance that enabled me to complete the manuscript. I am fortunate to have worked with Carol Goldberg of Doubleday & Co., Inc., a uniquely thoughtful editor who steered the manuscript through production with remarkable skill and dispatch. Unhappily, I am forced to absolve all individuals and institutions of responsibility for any shortcomings that may remain.

M. R.
Center for International Affairs
Harvard University
September 1972

Contents

Chapter 1

DEFINITION OF POLITICAL REVOLUTION

Few terms in contemporary English are used more ubiquitously—and more loosely—than "revolution." One reads about intellectual and artistic revolutions, economic and industrial revolutions, scientific and technological revolutions, social and cultural revolutions. One hears of revolutions in advertising, fashion, and hairdo. The list is virtually interminable.

Our concern in this book is far more limited: we are interested only in *political* revolution. We shall begin in this chapter by examining some current conceptions of revolution and then specifying their major weaknesses. We shall then be in a better position to propose a synthetic and, we hope, more adequate definition of political revolution.

A CRITIQUE OF CURRENT DEFINITIONS

Some current definitions of revolution emphasize its political/legal dimensions, others its social-systems attributes, and still others its psychological components. The political/legal definitions are perhaps the most common. They are exemplified in the work of Carl J. Friedrich, Eugene Kamenka, Raymond Tanter and Manus Midlarsky, George S. Pettee, Paul Schrecker, and Hannah Arendt.[1]

Friedrich defines political revolution simply "as a sudden

and violent overthrow of an established political order."[2] Kamenka believes that "revolution is a sharp, sudden change in the social location of political power, expressing itself in the radical transformation of the process of government, of the official foundations of sovereignty or legitimacy and of the conception of the social order. Such transformations . . . could not normally occur without violence, but if they did, they would still, though bloodless, be revolutions."[3] Tanter and Midlarsky hold that "a revolution may be said to exist when a group of insurgents illegally and/or forcefully challenges the governmental elite for the occupancy of roles in the structure of political authority. A successful revolution occurs when, as a result of the challenge to the governmental elite, insurgents are eventually able to occupy principal roles within the structure of political authority."[4]

Pettee and Schrecker stress the legal dimension. The former maintains that the most distinctive quality of revolutions is that they "always have changed the organization of government, and from this arises the common definition: a revolution is a change in the constitution by illegal means."[5] According to Schrecker, political revolution refers to "an illegal change of the constitution, or indeed, since the constitution *is* the system of norms which establishes the conditions of legality, as *an illegal change of the conditions of legality*."[6]

A unique conception of political revolution is developed by Hannah Arendt. Arendt defines revolution—in its most compelling dimension—as a "quest for freedom." Making a sharp distinction between freedom ("ability to do things") and liberation ("release from oppression"), Arendt maintains that revolution-as-a-quest-for-freedom is a modern phenomenon. There were no genuine revolutions before the eighteenth century. The American and French revolutions were "the first revolutions of freedom."[7]

Arendt is of course aware of the occurrence of other revolutions in recent times. She simply argues, however, that modern revolutions are prostitutions of freedom. In particular, she believes, the Marxian revolutions are perversions of freedom: they aim at material welfare and economic development ("the social question"), not freedom.

Arendt identifies two other components of a definition of revolution. One is the notion of newness, or novelty: "Crucial . . . to any understanding of revolutions in the modern age is that the idea of freedom and the experience of a new beginning should coincide."[8] Revolution, in other words, aims at freedom; the birth of freedom marks a new phase in history.

The third component of Arendt's definition is violence: freedom and novelty, she holds, cannot be brought forth except through violence. In sum, "only where change occurs in the sense of a new beginning, where violence is used to constitute an altogether different form of government, to bring about the formation of a new body politic, where the liberation from oppression aims at least at the constitution of freedom can we speak of revolution."[9]

The concept of revolution as a disequilibrium in the social system is associated primarily with Chalmers Johnson.[10] The problem of revolution, he maintains, must be approached in terms of social-systems theory. Revolutions must be studied in the context of the social systems in which they occur.

The distinguishing feature of a social system is equilibrium. There is no social system—indeed not any kind of system—unless there is equilibrium. A revolution, therefore, is a social system thrown out of equilibrium; it is a disequilibrated social system. Disequilibrium implies a breakdown of the system's roles, institutions, functions, and values.

In a 1964 work, Johnson attributed disequilibrium to "multiple dysfunctions" in the social system aggravated by the inability or unwillingness of the ruling elite to resolve them. Multiple dysfunctions and "elite intransigence" by themselves do not cause revolution, however. For a revolution to take place it is necessary that the dysfunctions be accelerated by a national crisis, such as defeat in war.[11]

In a later work, Johnson revised this formulation by

tracing disequilibrium to a breakdown of synchronization between the structure of social values and the pattern of change in the sociopolitical environment. Disequilibrium creates a condition of "power deflation" in which the ruling elite increasingly relies on force as a means of maintaining stability. Revolution occurs if the authority and legitimacy of the regime are destroyed as a consequence of the failure to introduce the adjustments necessary to accomplish a resynchronization. In the revised formulation, in short, power deflation plus loss of authority plus an accelerator account for revolution.[12]

Revolution means change, says Johnson, but a special kind of change: "True revolution is . . . the acceptance of violence in order to cause the system to change when all else has failed, and the very idea of revolution is contingent upon this perception of societal failure."[13]

The psychological approaches to revolution have been developed by Charles A. Ellwood, Peter H. Amann, Gustave Le Bon, and Dale Yoder, among others. According to these writers, the political, legal, and other definitions of revolution are deficient in that they emphasize the external manifestations of revolution at the expense of internal changes. These definitions see conflict, violence, and power transfer, but not the inner psychological dynamics in operation.

There is, according to Ellwood, a "psychic basis" of revolution, a universal psychological component through which all revolutions operate. Specifically, "revolutions are disturbances in the social order due to the sudden breakdown of social habits under conditions which make difficult the reconstruction of those habits, that is, the formation of a new social order. In other words, revolutions arise through certain interferences or disturbances in the normal process of the readjustment of social habits."[14]

Even under ordinary conditions, social habits and institutions undergo change; old habits and institutions are replaced by new ones—but all this is slow and gradual. (Ellwood views institutions as expressions of habits and customs.) Under revolutionary conditions, on the other hand, change is rapid and thorough; old habits and institutions suddenly lose their relevance. For Ellwood, this breakdown explains the anarchy in all revolutions: people have lost their frame of reference; behavior patterns have broken down.

If this theory is correct, Ellwood concludes, revolutions should be viewed as regular phenomena conforming to "the laws of the mental life."[15] As such, they should be predictable. In general, revolutions are more likely to occur when social habits and institutions are rigid and inflexible, when they do not change with changing times and conditions.

Analogous concepts of revolution are developed by Amann, Le Bon, and Yoder. According to Amann, for example, political regimes exist by virtue of two conditions: their monopoly of the means of physical force, and the existence of a widely shared "habit of obedience" among the masses. As such, a revolution is "a breakdown, momentary or prolonged, of the state's monopoly of power, usually accompanied by a lessening of the habit of obedience."[16]

Human society, Le Bon believes, rests on beliefs, sentiments, and myths. The "great revolutions" are those of manners and thought, those that transform the mentality of a people. "Whatever its origins, a revolution is not productive of results until it has sunk into the soul of the multitude."[17] Similarly Yoder holds, "The real revolution is the change in the social attitudes and values basic to the traditional institutional order."[18]

The foregoing definitions of revolution can be criticized on a number of grounds. The political/legal conceptions, for example, are unnecessarily permissive. Political revolution involves more than just illegal or violent change in government, state, or constitution. Moreover, if violence and illegality are considered the only defining criteria of revolution, then a wide range of phenomena—including some strikes—would qualify for inclusion.

Arendt's view of revolution as a quest for freedom is particularly constraining, to say nothing of its arbitrary

definition of "freedom." The American and the French
revolutions, Arendt would have us believe, are "revolutions of freedom," whereas the Algerian, Bolivian, and
Mexican revolutions, for example, are perversions of freedom. The obvious questions are: Whose freedom? From
whose point of view? By what criteria?

Moreover, Arendt's treatment involves a gross misrepre-
sentation of Marx. Marx's concern, as Arendt herself con-
cedes, was much broader than "the social question"; he
believed, among other things, that freedom and poverty
are incompatible. Nevertheless, Arendt proceeds to argue,
quite unconvincingly (except in a certain Hegelian sense),
that Marx's thought represents a surrender of freedom to
necessity.

The social-systems definition of revolution is too broad
and imprecise. Revolutions, one agrees, must be approached in the context of the society in which they occur,
but it is neither sufficient nor enlightening to view political
revolutions as social systems in disequilibrium. Johnson
does an excellent job of specifying some of the *conditions*
under which political revolution may occur (see Chapter
3, below), but he does not present a convincing *definition*
of political revolution. A related difficulty arises from the
fact that Johnson's approach represents an artificial linking
of revolution and the social system. The social-system concept throws little light on political revolution as such; indeed, it may unnecessarily complicate and hinder understanding. This approach may have potential utility for the
comparative analysis of political revolution, but much re-
finement remains to be introduced.

The psychological conceptions of revolution are particularly troublesome. For one thing, it may be rather
difficult, at any given time, to gauge accurately the extent to which "social habits" or "habits of obedience" have
broken down. Moreover, these conceptions confuse a definition of revolution with a statement of its causes or consequences. It is not clear, for example, whether a change
in social habits is a cause or an effect of revolution. Revolutions, as we shall see in Chapter 3, cannot be attributed

to any single cause. These and similar definitions simply specify one of many conditions under which revolutions may take place.

Finally, all three types of definition of revolution considered above share a serious conceptual difficulty: they obliterate any meaningful distinction between political revolution on the one hand, and coup d'état, riot, or rebellion on the other. To this topic we shall return in Chapter 2. For the moment, we simply note a need for greater precision and clarity in the treatment of these concepts.

We will summarize and highlight our criticism of the literature by citing a passage on revolution in which definition, cause, consequence, and types appear to be thoroughly confused:

> Revolution is used here as a general term to denote the wide range of circumstances—from mere threats of force to major civil wars [types of revolution?] —in which illegitimate violence is employed within a country to effect political change. . . . Revolutions have varied widely in purpose, scope, and intensity, but they have in common several characteristics which may serve as a basis for an introductory analysis: they result from a breakdown in the legitimate means of effecting political change [cause?]; they involve the use of illegitimate violence, from within or from without; they so disrupt the consensus necessary for the orderly conduct of society [cause? consequence?] that a major effort is required to legitimatize the policies of the victor; and they tend to become an issue in international relations [consequence?].[19]

A PROPOSED DEFINITION

Rather than setting down a definition of political revolution *ex cathedra*, we shall attempt to identify its major dimensions or components. The constituents of our definition are these:

1. At the most general level, revolution is a form of change.

2. This change is *relatively* abrupt, stretching perhaps over a period of two or three years to two or three decades.

3. This change is striking and far-reaching; it affects the behavior patterns of significant segments of the population.

These three components apply to all revolutions: intellectual, artistic, industrial, scientific, technological. To qualify as *political* revolution, an upheaval must meet five additional criteria:

4. Political revolution requires a mass movement. Although it is difficult if not impossible to be precise about the meaning of "mass," the intention here is to distinguish political revolution from other forms of violent action—say coup d'état or peasant rebellion (see Chapter 2). The component of mass makes revolution a modern phenomenon. We believe with Arendt—but for an entirely different reason—that the American and French revolutions represent the first "genuine" revolutions.

5. Revolutionary change is aimed *initially* at the political/governmental machinery. In this sense, political revolution involves a power transfer, a change in the distribution of political power, a transformation of the ruling class.

6. This power transfer aims at, seeks, or sets the stage for broader social change. Political revolution entails an array of disruptions on all fronts: political, economic, psychological, social.

7. Revolutionary change is illegal or extralegal. There are no "provisions" for it. It is "unauthorized."

8. Revolutionary change does not take place except through violence. Violence is a basic ingredient, a conspicuous quality of political revolution. This is because, among other things, change is resisted by the existing authorities. A "nonviolent political revolution" is a contradiction in terms.

Before turning to an elaboration of the nature and role of violence, with which political revolution is most frequently confused, we summarize the discussion by proposing the following definition: Political revolution refers to abrupt, illegal mass violence aimed at the overthrow of the political regime as a step toward over-all social change.[20]

It should perhaps be emphasized that all eight criteria discussed above are important constituents of the proposed definition; together they distinguish political revolution from other types of violent activity. Moreover, this definition accommodates successful as well as unsuccessful revolutionary movements; that is to say, one need *not* look at the outcome in order to identify the event. Finally, this definition makes political revolution not only a relatively modern but also a relatively rare phenomenon. In the sense here defined, political revolutions have been few in number; only a handful of political upheavals meet the criteria we have proposed. This realization is of course no drawback to analysis. In fact, in so far as it makes political revolution a distinctive phenomenon, it facilitates discussion and conceptualization. It also suggests that we need alternative terms for designating violent phenomena other than political revolution. To this topic we shall return in Chapter 2. Meanwhile, for stylistic reasons we shall at times employ the terms "revolution" and "political revolution" interchangeably throughout the volume.

POLITICAL REVOLUTION AND VIOLENCE

All revolution, we have said, entails violence. By violence is meant any behavior—physical or non-physical, direct or indirect, collective or individual—designed to injure, damage, or destroy persons or property.[21] The most common acts of violence are of course murder, assassination, riot, and any type of terrorist activity.

Violence comprises much more than physical acts, however. There is an important psychological dimension to violence, a dimension more subtle, brutal, and brutalizing than the physical. Terrorist activity, for example, may leave a profound psychological impact and create serious psychological insecurity. More important are those psychological acts of violence intended to deprive others of their personal integrity—or indeed of their humanity.

The most provocative discussion of psychological violence is offered by Frantz Fanon. Fanon's primary focus is the colonial situation and the way in which the colonizer dehumanizes and brutalizes the native and turns him into an animal. He writes:

> The settler paints the native as a sort of quintessence of evil. . . . The native is declared insensible to ethics; he represents not only the absence of values, but also the negation of values. He is, let us dare to admit, the enemy of values, and in this sense he is the absolute evil. He is the corrosive element, destroying all that comes near him; he is the deforming element, disfiguring all that has to do with beauty or morality; he is the depository of maleficent powers, the unconscious and irretrievable instrument of blind forces. . . .
>
> At times this Manicheism goes to its logical conclusion and dehumanizes the native, or to speak plainly, it turns him into an animal. In fact, the terms the settler uses when he mentions the native are zoological terms. He speaks of the yellow man's reptilian motions, of the stink of the native quarter, of breeding swarms, of foulness, of spawn, of gesticulations. When the settler seeks to describe the native fully in exact terms he constantly refers to the bestiary.[22]

According to Fanon, colonialism "is violence in its natural state, and it will only yield when confronted with greater violence. . . . The colonized man finds his freedom in and through violence."[23]

Violence is endemic in all society; there is nothing unnatural or pathological about it. Nieburg maintains that "Extreme and violent political behavior cannot be dismissed as erratic, exceptional, and meaningless. . . . Violence in all its forms . . . is a natural form of political behavior." He adds: "Until recently, the social sciences have conspicuously omitted to recognize or study seriously the political dynamics and dimensions of violent behavior except to treat it as aberrant and atypical, involving only backward nations and demented individuals."[24]

Violence saturates the fabric of social relationships. There are "legitimate" and institutionalized expressions of violence in all human society. Witness, for example, the pervasiveness of violence in organized sports, the governmental resort to violence in defense of "law and order," the routine exercise of violence in international politics, the ceremonial demonstration of a nation's capacity for violence in war games and military maneuvers.

It is useful to distinguish the actual exercise of violence from its potential use. Actual violence may not always be necessary to the realization of a given objective; the threat alone may prove sufficient. Some of the earliest insights in this regard are found in Georges Sorel, who emphasized the threat of violence—indeed, the "myth of violence"—as a means of accomplishing social goals. Myths, he writes, are "not descriptions of things, but expressions of a determination to act."[25] The most effective myth for Sorel is the myth of the general strike.

More modern thinkers, while recognizing the potential effectiveness of the threat of violence, have stressed the necessity of convincing opponents of one's ability to undertake actual violence to meet the exigencies of a given situation. Thus, for example, Nieburg emphasizes the importance of occasional demonstration of actual violence as a means of giving credibility to its potential use.[26] This, he states, gains efficacy for the threat of violence as an instrument of political and social change.

Violence may perform a number of important functions, both for individuals and for groups. "At the level of individuals," Fanon has forcefully argued, "violence is a cleansing force. It frees the native from his inferiority complex and from his despair and inaction; it makes him fearless and restores his self-respect."[27] Violence, in other words, is essential not only to the native's freedom but also to his psychological rehabilitation. Violence, Coser has maintained in a similar vein, is a psychological outlet for expressing anger, frustration, and discontent.[28]

Violence, some writers believe,[29] is necessary for the

preservation of national societies. Law, government, and bureaucracy all rest on violence or threat of violence. Moreover, violence or threat of violence serves to forge and preserve national identities. Violence tends to bind a society together: conflict with an out-group increases the solidarity of the in-group. Furthermore, violence helps dramatize grievances and injustices, bring them to public attention, and create a new social consciousness. By the same token, violence serves as a danger signal in human societies by focusing attention on the need for adjustment and accommodation. It tends to prevent stagnation of social systems by encouraging a progressive outlook and exerting pressure for innovation and change.

Violence has serious limitations. Those who undertake violence must consider factors of time, place, audience, and objective, as well as the relative strength of the opposition. They must know when to proceed and when to back off. Above all, the goals of violence must always be in the forefront of consciousness. There is a point at which violent means tend to defeat the ends they are intended to realize.

Violence (in act or threat) is a routine feature of human society, though obviously it varies in form, extent, and intensity. Violence is an indispensable ingredient of political revolution but not its only ingredient.

Chapter 2

TYPOLOGY OF POLITICAL REVOLUTION

This chapter examines and evaluates some typologies of political revolution. It distinguishes political revolution from a series of related concepts. And it sets forth a typology of its own, consistent with the definition proposed in Chapter 1.

A CRITIQUE OF CURRENT TYPOLOGIES

Among the most prominent typologies of revolution are those developed by Feliks Gross, George S. Pettee, Raymond Tanter and Manus Midlarsky, Chalmers Johnson, and James N. Rosenau.

Gross distinguishes four types of revolution:[1] (1) A "revolution from below" refers to a mass movement, in part spontaneous, which, developing slowly, eventually explodes in a cataclysmic upheaval leading to far-reaching political and social change. (2) A "revolution from above" is a planned, organized, non-spontaneous seizure of political power by a small group of armed men at the very top of the political structure. It entails a rapid take-over of the centers of governmental authority (for example, the ministries), of the means of violence, and of the media of communication and transportation. There is no intention, however, to introduce social change. (3) A "combined seizure" contains elements of both revolution from below and revolution from above: in a moment of mass unrest, a group of armed men seizes the political and governmental apparatus. (4) A "palace revolution" refers to a transfer of power, sometimes violent, within the ruling group. The seizure is engineered by a dissident faction within the elite (family or party, for example), not by an "outside" group such as the military. There is no intention to institute political or social change.

Pettee identifies a fivefold typology of revolutions,[2] three of which are similar or identical to Gross's categories. These are "great national revolution" (revolution from below), coup d'état (revolution from above), and palace revolution. Pettee's fourth category is rebellion, defined as an uprising against unjust rule, law, or government. The final type is "systemic revolution," by which Pettee means such grand historical transformations as those from city-state to empire, from empire to feudalism, from feudalism to the nation-state.

Tanter and Midlarsky set forth four explicit criteria for a typology of revolutions: degree of mass participation, duration of the upheaval, amount of domestic violence (as measured by the number of casualties, for example), and the goals of the insurgents. They identify four types of revolution:[3]

1. Mass revolution: characterized by high mass participation, fairly long duration, high domestic violence, and the introduction of basic political and social change. Examples include the French, Russian, Chinese, and Algerian revolutions.

2. Revolutionary coup: distinguished by low mass participation, short to moderate duration, low to moderate domestic violence, and the introduction of changes in the political structure but not in society. Examples given are the Nazi and Egyptian revolutions.

3. Reform coup: marked by very low mass participation, usually short duration, low domestic violence, and the introduction of moderate changes in the political system. Developments in Argentina in 1955, France and Pakistan in 1958, and Turkey in 1960 are cited as examples.

4. Palace revolution: characterized by absence of mass participation, very short duration, absence of domestic violence, and insignificant changes in the political structure. Examples include most Latin American coups.

Johnson identifies four criteria for a typology of revolutions: targets of revolution (whether the specific regime, the form of government, or the society at large), the identity of the revolutionaries (whether elite or mass), the ideology of the revolutionaries (whether reformist, nationalist, or messianic), and the timing of the revolution (whether spontaneous or calculated). He sets forth six types of revolution:[4]

1. The jacquerie: a spontaneous mass peasant uprising with the limited aim of purging the local or national elites. A jacquerie seeks certain reforms but not the overthrow of the political system. Examples include peasant uprisings in China.

2. The millenarian rebellion: similar to the jacquerie but with the added dimension of a utopian ideal inspired by a charismatic leader. An example would be the Taiping rebellion (1851–64).

3. The anarchistic rebellion: a nostalgic reaction to change, a romantic idealization of a bygone order, and an attempt to restore a pre-existing state of affairs. Examples include the Vendée rebellion (1793–96) and the Boxer rebellion (1899–1900).

4. The conspiratorial coup d'état: planned work of a small elite, leading to the replacement of one ruling group by another. Examples include coups in the Middle East and Latin America.

5. The Jacobin Communist revolution: a spontaneous mass movement aimed at total political and social transformation. Examples include the French and Russian revolutions.

6. The militarized mass insurrection: a calculated, planned national and social revolution based on guerrilla warfare and broad popular support. Examples include revolutions in Algeria, China, and Vietnam.

In a series of recent studies a group of scholars including Harry Eckstein and James N. Rosenau have attempted to elaborate upon the concept of "internal war." This concept, according to Eckstein, "denotes any resort to violence within a political order to change its constitution, rulers, or policies. It . . . does [not] mean quite the same thing as certain more commonly used terms, such as revolution, civil war, revolt, rebellion, uprising, guerrilla warfare, mutiny, jacquerie, coup d'état, terrorism, or insurrection. It stands for the genus of which the others are species."[5] In other words, internal war is an all-inclusive category embodying all types of violent activity, including revolution.

Rosenau has identified three ideal types of internal wars, recognizing the overlap among them.[6] "Personnel wars" are struggles over the occupancy of roles in the existing structures of political authority, with no aspiration on the part of the actors to introduce political or social change. "Authority wars" refer to struggles over the arrangement as well as the occupancy of roles in the structures of political authority (that is, replacement of one government by another), with no aspiration on the part of the actors to introduce general social change. "Structural wars" are struggles not only over the personnel and structures of political authority but also over far-reaching social change; they affect the entire political and social system.

Personnel wars, as Rosenau points out, are lowest with regard to social change; authority wars (which include personnel) occupy an intermediate position; and structural wars (which include both personnel and authority) rank highest.

Having examined these typologies, one is left with an uneasy feeling that none of them is particularly useful or discriminating. This is primarily due to the fact that none of them is based upon an adequate conception of political revolution. In virtually all these typologies, only one of the several categories meets the criteria of the definition we have developed in Chapter 1. This includes Gross's revolution from below, Pettee's great national revolution, Tanter-Midlarsky's mass revolution, and Rosenau's structural war. In Johnson's typology, two categories—the Jacobin Communist revolution and militarized mass insurrection—qualify as political revolution.

Gross's conception of revolution, as well as that of Tanter and Midlarsky, is broad enough to enable these writers to lump together political revolution and coup d'état. Pettee's approach permits him to combine political revolution, coup d'état, rebellion, and "systemic revolution" in the same typology. Johnson's treatment fuses revolution, coup d'état, riot, rebellion, and the jacquerie. The Eckstein-Rosenau view of internal war is so all-embracing as to embody everything from demonstration to civil war, palace revolution to guerrilla warfare—thereby bringing into question the very utility of the concept. One scholar, not discussed above, finds it possible even to speak of "one-man revolutions."[7]

We have no alternative but to conclude that there are no adequate typologies of political revolution. Many of the typologies discussed above are not classifications of political revolution as such but of *non*-revolution or, if one prefers, of concepts *related* to political revolution. It is only commonplace to suggest that coup d'état, rebellion, and riot are not—by definition—political revolution. Such notions as "revolution from above" and "palace revolution" are contradictions in terms. At best these typologies may be viewed as classifications of violent or illegal political activity. But violence and illegality, as we have seen, are only two of several components of political revolution.

We are left with a dual task: to sort out the various concepts related to political revolution, and to construct a typology of political revolution consistent with the definition previously developed.

CONCEPTS RELATED TO POLITICAL REVOLUTION

At least three concepts require clarification: riot, rebellion, and coup d'état.

A riot is a non-legal, non-routine, generally spontaneous group action, transitory in time, indefinite in place, voluntary or semivoluntary in membership, undertaken to express specific grievance and frustration. A riot does not have a well-defined membership; the participants—rich and poor, liberal and reactionary—are momentarily drawn together to redress a felt injustice.[8]

A rebellion is a fairly short-lived, sometimes spontaneous group action, without elaborate ideology or organization, involving a relatively small but fairly well-defined segment of the population. Examples include slave rebellions in the United States and peasant rebellions in China and Russia. Like a riot, a rebellion merely seeks to redress certain injustices, not to bring about political and social change. The rebels are prepared to accept constituted authority once their demands are met.

A coup d'état is a sudden, unexpected, illegal, potentially violent act intended to replace one set of rulers by another.[9] A coup involves the seizure of the governmental/political apparatus and the strategic centers of political power (for example, the military, the ministries, the communications media). As such, it is usually violent, but not necessarily and not always so. Examples of non-violent coups d'état include those in Egypt (1952), Algeria (1965), and Ghana (1966).

A coup is a quiet, secret affair. It does not involve the people but is presented to them as a *fait accompli*. The actors are usually public officials of some sort. In fact, one may identify two types of coups, depending on the officials involved. An *intraelite* coup (that is, a palace revolution) is a coup within the existing ruling group in which one faction overthrows another. Khrushchev's ouster by Brezhnev and Kosygin in 1964 is a fair example. An *interelite* coup is a coup from outside the existing ruling group, one in which the military is characteristically involved.

Regardless of type, coups differ from revolutions in at least three respects: they do not involve mass action, they may or may not aim at social change, and they may or may not be violent.

A PROPOSED TYPOLOGY

The typology offered below is based upon a single criterion: the target or targets of political revolution. The target, or "enemy," against which a political revolution is directed is its most distinctive characteristic. Such other criteria as the identity of the revolutionaries (elite or mass), the ideology of the revolutionaries (reformist or nationalist), and the timing of the revolution (spontaneous or calculated) are not quite as useful as one might suppose. The criterion of the identity of the revolutionaries, for example, is useless, because political revolutions, in the sense in which we have defined them, employ both elite and mass. The same may be said of the notion of timing, since political revolutions are neither exclusively spontaneous nor exclusively calculated (see below). The criterion of ideology is rather puzzling, especially when one considers Chalmers Johnson's categorization, for example, of "reformist" as a type of revolutionary ideology—a contradiction in terms. Such other criteria as degree of mass participation, amount of violence, and duration are not very discriminating either. The principal reason is that, using these criteria, one would be forced to the logical but unwarranted conclusion that the Chinese Revolution, for example, was *more* of a political revolution than, say, the French, because it took longer or involved a greater number of people or was more violent.

Employing the criterion of target, three types of political revolution may be identified: civil revolution, national revolution, and abortive revolution. By a civil revolution we mean mass violent overthrow of a domestic enemy, the replacement of one political regime by another, and the desire to introduce over-all social change. Examples include France (1789), Mexico (1910), Russia (1917), and Bolivia (1952).

The term "civil" simply suggests that the target of political revolution is an internal one. A civil revolution, it should be noted, is not the same as a civil war. If war is defined as a formal, organized military clash between two independent governments or states occupying separate territories (i.e., "external" forces), then civil war is a formal, organized military clash between two competing governments or political authorities or armed factions within the same territory (i.e., "internal" forces).

A national revolution aims at mass violent overthrow
of a foreign (external) power, a change in the political
system, the termination of foreign rule, and the institutionalization of social change. Examples include the Algerian, American, Chinese, Cuban, and Vietminh revolutions. A national revolution is frequently waged against
a foreign enemy as well as its domestic representative, or
"puppet." It is in fact both a war and a revolution un-
folding at the same time—a war because of the formal
armed clash involving a foreign government, a revolution because of the mass violence aimed at internal political and social change. As such, the concept of national
revolution is similar to that of "revolutionary war."

It should be stressed by way of clarification that, to the
extent to which the term "national" is conventionally used
to mean "nationwide," both civil and national revolutions
fit its perimeters. However, if we employ a clumsy expression in the interest of precision, a civil revolution is a
nationwide revolution targeted primarily against a domestic regime, while a national revolution is a nationwide
revolution targeted primarily against a foreign enemy.

An abortive revolution refers to the failure of the violent mass movement to reach its target, whether internal
or external. Reasons may include inept leadership, inadequate organization, failure of communication or planning,
suppression at the hands of the authorities. An abortive
revolution may be either civil or national. The Hungarian
Revolution of 1956, for example, was primarily targeted
against a foreign enemy, while the French Revolution of
1968 was primarily directed against a domestic regime.

Before concluding this section, it may be useful to identify provisionally a fourth possible type of political revolution: counterrevolution. Technically understood, a counterrevolution is mass violence designed to return to power
a political group or regime (whether domestic or foreign)
and to restore a pre-existing state of affairs. A counterrevolution, in other words, is a form of restoration.

A counterrevolution, it should be stressed, is a logical
and technical possibility, not necessarily a real one—hence
its provisional status. Examples are extraordinarily diffi-

cult to come by. Charles Tilly refers to the Vendée movement of 1793–96 as a counterrevolution, while Chalmers Johnson, as we have seen above, classifies it as an "anarchistic rebellion." Tilly himself identifies the Vendée variously as a "counterrevolution," a "revolt," a "rebellion," a "great rebellion," an "uprising," a "great uprising," an "insurrection," a "war," and a "great war."[10] Some scholars have identified among the motives of the Vendée the restoration of the monarchy or of the Church, while others have stressed the strong opposition to conscription. No simple assertion is possible, as Tilly points out, and a multiplicity of motives must be taken into account.

On the other hand, if the Revolutionary Peronist Movement (MONTONEROS) were to succeed in restoring Perón or Peronism in Argentina, that would come close to being a "model" of counterrevolution.

SUMMARY

In this chapter we have briefly examined and evaluated some prominent typologies of political revolution. We have set forth a typology of our own, consistent with the definition developed in the previous chapter, and we have attempted to distinguish political revolution from certain other, related concepts.

In developing our definition and typology, we have placed serious limitations upon the kinds of phenomena we can label "political revolution." This is inescapable, since the very acts of definition and classification are ambivalent ones, involving both inclusion and exclusion. On the one hand, they are intellectually liberating, because, if performed successfully, they throw light on otherwise obscure problems. On the other hand, they are intellectually constraining, in that they place limitations upon the kinds of phenomena to be observed and studied. Our objective in these two chapters has been simply to bring out the distinctiveness of political revolution as a generic concept and to delineate the forms it may take.

We are now in a position to proceed with an analysis

of the subject of strategy in political revolution. We shall subsequently test our conception of strategy in selected political revolutions corresponding to the typology developed in this chapter.

Chapter 3

THE STRATEGY OF POLITICAL REVOLUTION

CONDITIONS

Political revolutions do not occur haphazardly or fully spontaneously. A syndrome of variables coalesce before political revolutions take place. These variables are of two types: the "givens" and the "manipulables." The givens of political revolution—hereinafter labeled "conditions"—consist of an array of observable economic, political, social, and psychological changes or occurrences. These conditions themselves are of two sorts: (1) long-term factors that generate discontent and create a revolutionary environment, and (2) short-term factors that ignite a political revolution once the environment has been created. One scholar has conveniently labeled the former "preconditions" and the latter "precipitants."[1]

The manipulables of political revolution—hereinafter called "strategy"—refer in essence to the skill, commitment, and resourcefulness of the revolutionaries to fashion all necessary tools and undertake all necessary activity toward the realization of their objectives. Strategy entails the manipulation of conditions (the givens), to be sure, just as conditions have a bearing on strategy, but the two are analytically distinct.

The conditions of political revolution have been elaborated with considerable brilliance by a number of scholars, including Crane Brinton, James C. Davies, Harry Eckstein, Ivo K. and Rosalind L. Feierabend, Ted Robert Gurr, Chalmers Johnson, George S. Pettee, Raymond Tanter and Manus Midlarsky, and others. We do not intend a detailed examination of the theoretical formulations and empirical findings of these scholars at this juncture. However, inasmuch as conditions may either facilitate or impede strategy, we will briefly classify and present them in propositional outline form. In the classification that follows, a degree of arbitrariness has been unavoidable.

I. Preconditions of Political Revolution[2]
  A. Economic
    1. Adversity: The most important precondition of political revolution is the progressive deterioration of economic conditions (Marx and others).
    2. Prosperity: Political revolution occurs under conditions of relative economic prosperity (de Tocqueville, Brinton, Edwards, Pettee).
    3. Adversity preceded by prosperity: Political revolutions are most likely to occur when a prolonged period of economic prosperity is followed by a brief period of sharp reversal, thus creating an intolerable gap between expected need satisfaction (aspiration) and actual need satisfaction (achievement) (Davies, Tanter-Midlarsky).
  B. Psychological
    1. Discontent, frustration: The most basic precondition of political revolution (as of all types of violence) is relative deprivation, defined as men's perception of discrepancy between their value expectations (aspiration) and value capabilities (achievement) (Gurr; *cf.* Feierabend and Feierabend). However, whether relative deprivation explodes into actual violence is a function of two sets of intervening variables: (a) the scope and intensity of normative (historical, cultural, ideological) justifications for violence as well as men's perception of the effectiveness and utility of violence in solving social problems; (b) the relative physical strength of the contending parties as well as their ability to provide institutionalized, peaceful alternatives to violent expression of discontent (Gurr).

2. Alienation: A revolutionary movement is most likely to emerge when large numbers of people are alienated from the sociopolitical system, when tension and uncertainty are heightened as a result of a real or perceived "loss of community," and when there is an insurgent appeal to recapture community through revolutionary action (Schwartz and others).

C. Political

1. Foreign control: Whether in the form of alien (dynastic) rule or imperialist penetration, foreign control sets off revolutionary movements when people attain sufficient consciousness to realize that they can act to change the conditions of oppression and exploitation under which they live (Leiden-Schmitt and others).

2. Governmental inefficiency: In prerevolutionary societies, governments are in bad financial and administrative straits. The taxation system is inadequate; the treasury is nearly depleted; bribery and corruption are rampant; the administrative machinery is out of date; the bureaucracy is neither open nor responsive to public demands (Brinton and others).

3. Disintegration of the ruling elite: The ruling elite is inept; it has lost the skill to rule; it is faction ridden and open to coups (Brinton and others).

4. Elite intransigence: As criticism mounts, the ruling elite, instead of responding to the need for change, relies on a policy of increasing repression, thus channeling all discontent into violent behavior (Johnson).

D. Social

1. Ideological decay: The dominant ideology (including the system of social norms and values) is in a state of decline; it is losing force and relevance; it is challenged by powerful alternative ideologies (Pettee and others).

2. Institutional decay: Practices and behavior patterns are increasingly out of joint with reality; a

rigidly ascriptive social structure prevents new
classes and groups from advancement; there is discrepancy between economic position and sociopolitical status (Pettee and others).

3. Social disequilibrium: A breakdown of sychroni-
zation between the pattern of values and the direction of sociopolitical change challenges the authority and legitimacy of the regime (Johnson).

4. Class antagonisms: Class antagonisms—though not
necessarily of the Marxian variety—grow more intense; class distinctions are increasingly viewed as
unnatural, immoral, and unjust (Brinton and
others).

5. The desertion of the intellectuals: The intellectuals
begin to turn away from the regime, undermine
its effectiveness and legitimacy, and propagate alternative visions of society (Brinton, Edwards).

II. Precipitants of Political Revolution[3]

A. Certain events—for example, war, army mutiny, coup
d'état, palace revolution—may deprive the ruling
regime of its weapons of violence.

B. The revolutionaries may take awesome risks based
on a messianic belief in the inevitability of success;
they may believe, for example, that an attack upon
the regime will bring forth a crippling general strike.

C. The revolutionaries may conduct special operations
against the regime, such as guerrilla or terrorist activity.

D. Historical accidents may set off revolutionary movements—for example, the accidental explosion of a
bomb in the revolutionaries' warehouse in Hankow
on October 10, 1911.

The conditions of political revolution, then, are varied
and complex, and in some cases mutually contradictory
(for example, elite ineptitude versus elite intransigence).
No revolution is likely to exhibit all these conditions, nor
is such a stipulation necessary. However, it is important
to avoid monistic explanations of political revolution, such

as the notion that political revolution is simply a consequence of economic changes or that it is brought forth by the conspiracies of a minority of wicked men.

THE CONCEPT OF STRATEGY

The manipulables of political revolution, considered collectively, shall be labeled "strategy." The concept of strategy underlying this book is necessarily broader than the traditional approaches to that term. The word "strategy," in its original Greek meaning as "the art of the general," betrayed an exclusively military preoccupation, much of which has been carried over to modern times.[4] Clausewitz defined strategy as "the art of the employment of battles as a means to gain the object of war. In other words strategy forms the plan of the war, maps out the proposed course of the different campaigns which compose the war, and regulates the battles to be fought in each."[5] The British military writer B. H. Liddell Hart has developed a threefold conception of strategy: (1) "Pure or military strategy" is "a sound calculation and coordination of the end and the means." (2) "Strategy" as a generic concept refers to "the art of distributing and applying military means to fulfill the ends of policy." (3) "Grand or higher strategy" is "policy in execution"; it coordinates and directs "all the resources of a nation, or band of nations, towards the attainment of the political objective of the war—the goal defined by fundamental policy."[6] In an elaboration on Liddell Hart, the French military theorist André Beaufre approaches strategy as "the art of applying force so that it makes the most effective contribution towards achieving the ends set by political policy. . . . In my view the essence of strategy is the abstract interplay which . . . springs from the clash between opposing wills. . . . It is therefore the art of the dialectic of force or, more precisely, *the art of the dialectic of two opposing wills using force to resolve their dispute.*"[7]

The American military writer J. C. Wylie has attempted

to develop a general theory of strategy applicable to all conflict situations, not just war. He isolates what he thinks is the single factor "common to all struggles, military and nonmilitary. This common factor is the concept of control, some form or degree or extent of control exercised by one social entity over another." The principal means employed are "the manipulations of the center of gravity of the situation." As for military strategy, "The primary aim . . . in the conduct of war is some selected degree of control of the enemy for the strategist's own purpose; this is achieved by control of the pattern of war; and this control of the pattern of war is had by manipulation of the center of gravity of war."[8]

The foregoing approaches view strategy broadly as the conceptualization, planning, and direction of war, by top military commanders, consistent with overriding political objectives. They usually distinguish strategy from tactics, the latter understood as specific battlefield operations consistent with the over-all plan and handled by lesser, field commanders. Wylie's attempt to develop a general theory of strategy must be rated unsuccessful, since the concepts of "control" and "manipulation of centers of gravity" are too general to be operationally useful. His effort boils down to an end/means analysis without shedding additional light on the subject of strategy.

Military strategy is certainly an important component of the strategy of political revolution, but not the whole of it. For our purposes, strategy is defined, at the most general level, as the over-all plan for the operationalization, implementation, direction, and control of the manipulables of political revolution. Strategy refers to all actions, policies, instruments, and apparatus necessary for mounting a revolutionary upheaval. It entails the deployment of men, matériel, ideas, symbols, and forces in pursuit of revolutionary objectives. Specifically, as used in this book, strategy has five principal components: leadership, ideology, organization, the use of terror and violence, and the manipulation of the international situation. Each will be considered in turn.

LEADERSHIP

A corps of competent leaders is manifestly indispensable to any political revolution. This corps is ordinarily supplemented by a charismatic leader: an individual with seemingly superhuman qualities and an ability to command a hypnotic hold over the masses.

A number of studies have been made of revolutionary leadership. Some of these studies are speculative, focusing on various types of leaders and their functions in various phases of revolution. Other studies focus on empirical analyses of characteristics, social backgrounds, education, and occupation of revolutionary leaders.

Among the best known of the speculative studies is one by Eric Hoffer, in which three types of revolutionary leaders, corresponding to three successive stages of revolutionary development, are identified.[9] Political revolutions, according to Hoffer, are prepared by the "men of words," brought to a head by the "fanatic," and consolidated by the "practical men of action." The men of words lay the groundwork for revolution by discrediting the prevailing creeds and institutions, creating a hunger for a new faith or ideology, and undermining the confidence of the ruling regime.

When the revolutionary movement is ripe, only the fanatic can lead it. The men of words are unsuitable for the violent struggles of revolution; the crumbling of the old regime frightens them out of their wits. "Not so the fanatic. Chaos is his element. When the old order begins to crack, he wades in with all his might and recklessness to blow the whole hated present to high heavens."[10]

The essential qualities of the fanatic are: (1) audacity —an utter disregard for impediments and a sheer joy in defiance; (2) blind faith in a holy cause; (3) personal magnetism, to attract a large following; (4) an understanding that the greatest craving of the followers is for unity, solidarity, communion; and (5) ability to attract a devoted group of able lieutenants. Hoffer also identifies some qualities the fanatic does *not* need: exceptional intelligence, noble character, originality. In fact, Hoffer thinks, these may be impediments.[11]

Political revolutions, according to Hoffer, are consolidated by the practical men of action: the reasonable, coolheaded men who institutionalize and sanctify the revolution. They have the ability to bargain, compromise, and negotiate in an effort to restore a semblance of stability. They can sense the direction of social forces and sentiments and adjust their behavior accordingly.

It is usually advantageous to the movement, Hoffer maintains, that these three roles be played by different men in successive stages of revolution. This has the effect of enhancing the dynamism and efficiency of the movement. Few men, Hoffer points out, have the ability to play all three roles effectively. In fact, he believes, the Fascist and Nazi movements (not "revolutions" in our definition) failed in part because Mussolini and Hitler were unable to adjust to their roles as practical men of action.

A similar conception of revolutionary leadership has been developed by Rex D. Hopper, who identifies four types of leaders in four successive stages of political revolution.[12] In the "preliminary" stage, leadership belongs to the agitator, the man who seeks to bring awareness to the masses, highlight abuses and injustices, maximize restlessness and discontent, and challenge the entire fabric of society. In the stage of "popular involvement," leadership belongs to the prophet and the reformer—the prophet because he has special knowledge and a special sense of mission, the reformer because he attacks specific issues and offers specific alternatives and programs. In the "formal" stage of political revolution, leadership is in the hands of the statesmen: those who can formulate and operationalize new policy and gauge popular demands and desires. The last, or "institutional," stage of the movement sees the emergence of the administrators and executives: technicians who create new institutional arrangements for the realization of revolutionary goals.

These and similar studies,[13] while intrinsically interesting, do not tell us much about the actual characteristics of revolutionary leaders. To fill this gap we must turn to empirical findings concerning leaders of revolutionary movements. The major problem in this connection is a lamentable lack of social background data. The available information is summarized as follows:

Age. Revolutionary leaders, it appears, are neither very young nor very old. Crane Brinton has found, for example, that the leaders of the English, French, American, and Russian revolutions were in their thirties and forties.[14] George K. Schueller fixes the average age of the Bolshevik Politburo members in 1917 at thirty-nine.[15] Robert C. North and Ithiel de Sola Pool put the average age of the members of the Chinese Politburo in the 1920s as ranging between twenty-seven and thirty-three, and the average age of the Kuomintang leaders as just over forty.[16] Ming T. Lee discovers that of the fifty-two founders of the Chinese Communist Party (CCP) in 1921, 94 per cent were forty years of age or under and 73 per cent thirty years of age or under.[17] Robert A. Scalapino reports the average age of Asian Communist leaders in 1965 as between forty and fifty-five.[18]

Social and Occupational Background. Revolutionary leaders are broadly middle class in origin. The English, American, and French revolutions, for example, were thoroughly bourgeois affairs, led by prominent members of the middle (and, in some cases, upper) class. Brinton reports that among the fifty-six signers of the Declaration of Independence were five physicians, twenty-two lawyers, three ministers, and eleven merchants; and that nearly all were affluent.[19]

The middle-class character of revolutionary leadership is equally true of Communist leaders. Schueller has documented the middle-class origins of a substantial number of the Bolshevik Politburo members.[20] Lee has found that of the fifty-two founders of the CCP, over 90 per cent had middle-class backgrounds and were engaged in middle-class occupations.[21] Scalapino reports that Asian revolutionary leaders come predominantly from the bourgeoisie (particularly the lower bourgeoisie), and that a majority are active in middle-class occupations.[22] John H. Kautsky has discovered that of a sample of thirty-two revolutionary leaders of the Third World, fully thirty (93 per cent) occupy middle- and upper-middle-class positions in law, medicine, journalism, education, or government bureaucracy.[23]

In short, both the lower class (whether proletariat or peasantry) and the upper class are underrepresented in political revolutions, the former because it usually lacks the necessary talent and skill, the latter because it is usually antirevolutionary.

Place of Origin. Revolutionary leaders usually come from urban settings, as their middle-class backgrounds would virtually require. Prominent exceptions include Mao Tse-tung and Ho Chi Minh.

Education. Revolutionary leaders are far better educated than the average population. It is a commonplace that revolutionary leaders are drawn most characteristically from the intelligentsia. Brinton has found, for example, that of the fifty-six signers of the Declaration of Independence, thirty-three held college degrees, and only four or five had little or no formal education.[24] Scalapino reports that most Asian Communist leaders have had some higher education and that many can be described as "intellectuals."[25] Kautsky discovers that in his sample of thirty-two revolutionary leaders of the Third World, twenty-five (78 per cent) had received university or advanced professional training, and eighteen (56 per cent) had lived or traveled extensively abroad.[26] Lee finds that of the fifty-two founders of the CCP 42 per cent were college graduates, while 82 per cent had had at least some college education, and 96 per cent had either resided abroad or experienced the "new style" of education.[27]

Regardless of type, age, social background, occupation, and education, revolutionary leaders must demonstrate an ability to perform certain fundamental tasks. Minimally, they must devise an appropriate ideology, create an appropriate organization, employ effective terror and violence, and manipulate the international situation to maximum advantage.

IDEOLOGY

Every revolution has a great myth or ideology. Ideology may be defined as an emotion-laden, myth-saturated, action-related system of beliefs and values.[28] An important feature of ideology is an appeal to emotion, an eliciting of an affective response. The myths and values of ideology are communicated through symbols in an efficient and economical manner. Symbols capture large expanses of meaning and communicate this meaning instantaneously.

Ideology relies on normative judgments. Every ideology is based in part on a denunciation of the existing order through an appeal to normative and moral principles. Moral protest, moral indignation, moral outrage are all indispensable to any ideology. Moreover, ideologies set forth positive values of their own: liberty, equality, humanity, classless society.

Ideology entails an element of distortion or myth. The values or goals of ideology are characteristically inflated out of proportion to reality; there is no necessary correspondence between ideology and reality.

The goals and values of ideology are embodied in a program of action. Ideology seeks to relate specific patterns of action to the realization of goals and values. Some ideologies may contain a statement of priorities specifying immediate, intermediate, and ultimate goals.

Ideology may perform a number of crucial social-psychological functions. First, it articulates social ills, denounces existing ideas and institutions, and undermines the confidence and morale of the ruling regime while simultaneously offering an alternative set of values and a new vision of society. Second, ideology rationalizes, legitimizes, and justifies the grievances and demands of the revolutionaries; it lends dignity to revolutionary action. Third, ideology gives the revolutionaries a sense of unity, solidarity, and cohesion; it instills revolutionary zeal, commitment, devotion, and sacrifice. Fourth, ideology serves as an instrument of mass mobilization. The revolutionary leadership must go among the masses, capitalize on their malaise and discontent, capture their trust and confidence, rally them to the cause, and actively involve them in revolution. The greater the revolutionaries' skill in mobilizing and politicizing the masses, and the greater their ability to create an atmosphere of popular commitment, the greater their chances of success.

Finally, ideology may serve as a cover for personal motives and ambitions of the revolutionary leaders. The elite is always in a position to employ ideology to manipulate and control the masses. Indeed, one scholar writes, "ideologies are the crucial lever at the disposal of elites for obtaining mass mobilization and for maximizing the possibilities of mass manipulation. That is . . . the single major reason that ideology is so important to us."[29]

Any discussion of ideology must take into account the principle of ideological dilution. The point is that if a revolution is to succeed, the ideology must have wide popular appeal. If it is to capture such appeal, the ideology must be diluted. The ideology, in other words, must be flexible and opportunistic. The position of the ideology on various issues cannot be fixed and final; it must leave ample room for maneuver and compromise. Ideological purism may prove fatal.

ORGANIZATION

Organization is a fundamental adjunct to ideology, the link between ideology and action. The leadership translates ideology into action through the medium of organization. Ideology helps "reach" the masses; organization functions to tap their energies and channel them toward the realization of revolutionary objectives. Philip Selznick writes: "Although ideology, to be translated into power, requires organization, effective organization also requires ideology."[30] He quotes Lenin to the effect that organization is the only effective weapon in the hands of the revolutionary class: "The proletariat can become and inevitably will become a dominant force only because its intellectual unity created by the principles of Marxism is fortified by the material unity of organization which welds millions of toilers into an army of the working class."[31] Samuel P. Huntington has laid down as a general principle that "Organization is the road to political power. . . . In the modernizing world [as elsewhere?] he controls the future who organizes its politics."[32] Organization is the key to effective communication and intelligence operations, both crucial in revolutionary action.

Organization takes two broad forms—political and military. Political organization takes the form of political clubs, political societies, study groups, and, most significantly, political parties. The revolutionary party is typically (though not always) an elitist organization. The business of revolution, as Lenin put it, can be entrusted only to those who have devoted their entire life to revolution, that is, to the "professional revolutionaries."[33] What is needed is skill and ability, not numbers—quality not quantity.

What the party lacks in numbers it compensates for in single-mindedness, determination, and devotion to the cause. There must be relentless pursuit of revolutionary objectives, an ability to lead a spartan life, a willingness to risk one's own peace and security.

Small numbers have the further advantage of facilitating discipline and control. The revolutionary party is typically centralized, tightly knit, and closely controlled. Without discipline and control cohesion and solidarity will be undermined; without cohesion and solidarity no revolution can hope to succeed. Therefore, revolutionary organizations tend to be anti-democratic. There is little tolerance of disagreement, little provision for dissent, little respect for minority views.

Every revolution requires a military force, an army to fight the battles that need to be fought. The military organization, at least initially, need not be too extensive. Communist theoreticians, in particular, believe that a small number of individuals—as small as thirty or forty—can initiate a revolutionary movement. Mao Tse-tung boasted in an interview with Edgar Snow, for example, that the Chi-

nese People's Liberation Army started with a few dozen
ill-equipped peasants.[34] Che Guevara has expressed the
opinion that "a nucleus of 30 to 50 men is sufficient to
initiate an armed fight in any country of the Americas."[35]
Fidel Castro has maintained that a revolutionary struggle
can be launched by "four, five, six, or seven" guerrillas.[36]
Indeed, guerrilla warfare is an attempt to show that a small
band of determined revolutionaries can mount a decisive
struggle against the superior forces of the established regime.

Traditionally, in both Communist and non-Communist
thought, the military has been an instrument in the hands
of the party and subservient to the party. Mao and Lenin,
for example, would insist on the complete subordination
of the military to political organization, and they would
employ political cadres and commissars to institutionalize
this arrangement. In recent times a serious challenge to
this view has been mounted by some writers on revolution,
particularly in the context of the Cuban experience. To
this topic we shall return in Chapter 7.

THE ROLE OF TERROR AND VIOLENCE

We may define terror as any act designed to influence
political behavior by extranormal means—for example, by
generating fear, uncertainty, anxiety, and insecurity. Terror necessarily involves the actual use or the threat of
violence. According to Walter, "the first element of the
terror process . . . is the specific act or threat of violence,
which induces a general psychic state of extreme fear,
which in turn produces typical patterns of reactive behavior."[37] Terrorist activity includes acts of murder, subversion, sabotage, destruction of public property, spreading rumors of impending chaos, throwing bombs into
restaurants and theaters.

Terror is of two broad types: revolutionary (launched
by the insurgents) and governmental (launched by the
incumbents). A distinction between terror and counter-
terror made on this basis is farfetched, however, since it

assumes that governmental terror is always launched in response to revolutionary terror. The initiation of terror by government is by no means an uncommon experience. Chiang Kai-shek's China, Batista's Cuba, and Duvalier's Haiti are classic examples.[38]

Revolutionary terror may perform a number of important functions:[39] First, it advertizes and popularizes the movement. Second, it builds morale and confidence within the revolutionary camp. Third, it helps bring out and crystallize the various factions in the revolution—the pro, the con, and the undecided—and facilitate the adoption of an appropriate policy toward each faction. Fourth, it provokes governmental terror, which, since the revolutionaries are likely to be elusive, will tend to be indiscriminate and repressive, thus further alienating the population. The most important functions of terror, however, are political/psychological, not military. Terror is not intended to win the revolutionary struggle as such, but to undermine enemy morale by creating an atmosphere of disorientation, chaos, fright, anxiety, and despair. Terror is designed to so shock, numb, and demoralize the people and the enemy as to make them eager to compromise for the sake of relaxation of tensions and the return of an atmosphere of "normalcy."

MANIPULATION OF THE INTERNATIONAL SITUATION[40]

The inclusion of this component of strategy arises from the realization that domestic and international politics are closely intertwined, that political revolutions influence, and are in turn influenced by, the balance of international forces. Few revolutionary movements have been unaffected by the international situation; few have succeeded or failed exclusively on their own.

There are certain mechanisms or dynamics inherent in the nature of political revolution that work to "externalize" or "internationalize" it. These mechanisms are found in the foreign operations and activities of both the insurgents and the incumbents as the two groups compete for

international support. The party that succeeds in isolating
the other has a better chance of winning the struggle.

Specifically, since the insurgents are almost always
weaker than the incumbents, one way for them to neutralize the latter and to continue their own existence is to appeal for foreign support. Such support may include funds,
arms, supplies, and manpower. The most important form
of support, however, is a foreign base of operation (a
sanctuary), preferably in a contiguous country.

The insurgents' appeal for outside support is typically
counterbalanced by the incumbents' counterappeal. This
taking of countermeasures for international aid is usually
easier for the incumbents, since they are in formal control
of the political and diplomatic apparatus of the country
and since they are likely to have a variety of international
contacts.

In this fashion an "internal" struggle is internationalized.
Political revolution becomes a matter of international
concern, diplomacy, and maneuvering. The appeals and
counterappeals may influence international alignments and
generate conflict.

There is a second series of dynamics that tends to turn
a political revolution into an international event. Inherent
in the nature of the international system is a "culture," or
"climate of opinion." This culture, or opinion, may do one
of three things: (1) It may help strengthen the incumbents
and bolster their confidence, bring sanctions against
the insurgents, deny them respectability, and isolate and
suppress them. Examples include international opinion toward Communist insurgency in Malaya, the Philippines,
and Korea. (2) International culture may favor the insurgents, boost their morale, feed their hopes, facilitate the
flow of supplies and funds, and isolate and demoralize the
incumbents. Examples include international attitudes toward anti-colonial movements in various parts of Africa.
(3) International opinion may favor neither the incumbents nor the insurgents but seek instead reconciliation and
avoidance of potentially cataclysmic violence. An example
would be Laos in the 1960s.

The fate of the revolution, then, depends in part on the

international balance of forces, and on international culture and opinion, at a given point in time. It is thus incumbent upon revolutionary leadership accurately to gauge these variables and to attempt to manipulate them with the greatest possible efficiency. Such manipulation is never easy, to be sure, but every effort must be made to lay the groundwork for capturing international support, both material and spiritual. This may be done by diluting the movement's ideological posture—even by deliberately slanting the ideology—to appeal to specific foreign countries and to the international system in general. Minimally, every effort must be made to neutralize foreign support for the incumbents.

SUMMARY

In this chapter we have discussed the strategy of political revolution in terms of five principal components. We have seen not only the importance of leadership, ideology, organization, terror, and the international situation, but also their close interrelationships. Revolutionary leaders must have the ability to devise appropriate ideology and organization, employ terror and violence, and manipulate the international situation. Leadership, ideology, and organization are quite literally intertwined. Without competent leadership both ideology and organization are likely to remain ineffectual. Without organization ideological mobilization is likely to collapse; without ideology mass mobilization will not get off the ground. Ideology helps capture respectability for the revolution, its leaders, its activities, its goals and objectives. Effective leadership and organization make possible effective deployment of terror and violence; effective ideology helps justify it. Effective leadership and flexible ideology help maximize the international appeal of the revolution.

In Part II we will apply this concept of strategy to three political revolutions to determine its usefulness or validity. Selected in the context of the typology developed in Chapter 2, the three revolutions took place in Bolivia (1952), Vietnam (1946–54), and France (1968). The se-

lection of these revolutions is governed by the criteria out-
lined in the Preface, and by the interests of the investigator.
Although space limitation does not permit application of
our framework to other cases, we believe our theoretical
approach equally valid for the analysis of other revolutionary movements.[41]

Having tested our conception of strategy against empirical data from three revolutions, we will turn, in Part III,
to a synthesis of our efforts.

Part II

APPLICATION

Chapter 4

CIVIL REVOLUTION: BOLIVIA

The desire for national integration and unity, the demand for social justice and political equality, the need for a redistribution of the national wealth—these dynamics shaped the Bolivian Revolution. Although integration entailed considerable reliance on nationalism, this nationalism was directed *primarily* toward domestic construction, not against a colonial power. Economically Bolivia was heavily dependent on foreign businessmen and foreign trade, but politically, socially, and culturally it had remained free of imperialist infringement since its attainment of independence from Spain, in 1825.

CONDITIONS

The Bolivian Revolution of 1952 was a response to a series of military, political, economic, and social/psychological conditions set in motion or exacerbated by the Chaco War, 1932–35.

Prior to 1952 Bolivia was a "land divided," a society of extreme separation. The Indians found their place at the lowest level of the Bolivian social hierarchy. Although they comprised approximately 50 per cent of the total population of around three million, the Indians played no role in the nation's civil or political life. A number of interwoven factors contributed to the powerlessness of the Indians. Living in the countryside, they were far removed from the centers of political activity in the cities. Lacking schools, the countryside produced a largely illiterate population; and yet literacy was a requirement for voting. The lack of schools had another consequence: the Indians had little opportunity to learn Spanish, the nation's official language and another prerequisite of political participation. Religion, like language, separated the Indians from national life; through a transparent veneer of Catholicism, they worshipped their ancestral gods. Poverty and stagnation dominated life in the countryside.

The Spanish had left their successors a sound legacy for keeping the Indians in line. Under the long and harsh Spanish rule, the Indian population had been converted to a belief in the supremacy of the white race and the invincibility of the white army. The initial consequence of the Indian's resignation to his social and psychological status was the creation of a closed society into which he retreated. Accompanying this retreat was a loss of pride, initiative, and creativity. In the words of a Bolivian minister of education:

> The Indian is a sphinx. He inhabits a hermetic world. . . . We don't understand his forms of life, nor his mental mechanism . . . we are ignorant of his individual psyche and his collective drama. The Indian lives. The Indian acts and produces. The Indian does not allow himself to be understood, he doesn't desire communication. Retiring, silent, immutable, he inhabits a closed world. The Indian is an enigma.[1]

A similar description has been offered by a Bolivian minister of foreign affairs:

> Uncommunicative and imperturbable, the Indian today remains in his centuries-old isolation. He is sober, tenacious, stoic in the face of physical and moral suffering. He speaks only his own language, Quechua or Aymará. Bronze-hued and beardless, rugged of features, squat and burly, the Bolivian Indian seems a part of the soil itself. It is difficult to picture

him against any background other than that of his
native earth. In the city he is a transient, a stranger.
. . . He lives in a hut consisting of four mud walls
and a thatched roof. He has no furniture—neither
beds, chairs, tables nor rugs. On the hard floor are
a few blankets, woven by his own hands, where he
sleeps the sleep of an exhausted animal.[2]

Just above the Indians in the Bolivian social structure
came the *mestizos,* or persons of mixed blood. Constituting
about 35 per cent of the population, the *mestizos* had acquired some occupational competence and held minor com-
mercial and administrative posts. The *mestizos* were
distinguished from the *cholos:* supposedly pure Indians
who had migrated to the cities as laborers, vendors, or domestic servants. Neither *mestizos* nor *cholos* had any political rights or privileges.

The upper extreme of the Bolivian social spectrum was
reserved for the country's white population of European
descent. Constituting about 15 per cent of the total population, this class comprised "a small circle" that dominated
Bolivia's "economy, politics, and culture."[3] Living in the
cities, educated in their own schools, and speaking Spanish,
members of this class monopolized power and wealth. They
viewed the Indians as constitutionally "ignorant" (due to
"Indian blood") and as "subhuman beings"; they required
the Indian "to get police permission to walk on the streets
of La Paz."[4] Aware of the status it had forced upon the
Indian population, the white upper class lived in constant
fear of an Indian insurrection.

The two extremes of Bolivian society were linked economically in mining and agriculture. Most Indians tilled
the land, with only about sixty thousand working the
mines. Minerals constituted 95 per cent of the country's
exports, of which tin accounted for about 70 per cent.
About 2 per cent of the population, the miners produced
virtually all of the country's export income.

The three giant enterprises of Simón Patiño, Mauricio
Hochschild, and Carlos Aramayo controlled approximately
75 per cent of the Bolivian mines. The "foreign tin barons,"

as they were called, regularly removed their profits from the country, investing much of their capital abroad. Patiño and Aramayo were Bolivians, but they were considered foreigners because, having made their fortunes in Bolivia, they spent most of their time in Europe and North America. All three companies were owned in substantial part by foreign concerns (see below).

Working in the mines meant low wages, bad conditions, absence of safety measures, a high probability of contracting silicosis or tuberculosis, and proximity to coercion and intimidation in the interest of greater profits. The Indians confronted daily repression inflicted upon them by men whose fear of an Indian insurrection served to justify further repression. The whites were determined to amass all wealth before their rule was terminated by a mass uprising.

Bolivia's agricultural establishment came close to being a model of medieval European feudalism. According to a 1950 census, 6.3 per cent of the population (all white) owned 92 per cent of the country's privately owned agricultural land, while 69.4 per cent of the farmers held only 0.4 per cent of the land.[5] Under this arrangement, the whites played landlords and the Indians serfs.

The Indian was sometimes called a sharecropper, but this term does not accurately reflect his status. The Indian was allotted a small plot of land on which to build a shelter, grow crops, and maintain a few animals. In return, he was obligated to the landlord for up to six days of labor each week. He also rendered compulsory personal service (*pongueaje*) as a servant in the landlord's house or a keeper of his stable. He could even be rented out to other landlords. The wife of the Indian—and frequently other members of his family as well—was required to serve as cook or maid, or to care for cattle or sheep. While performing personal service, the Indian and his family were expected to provide their own food and fuel.

The feudal system had dire consequences for Bolivian agriculture. Neither the landlord nor the Indian was predisposed to invest, innovate, or increase productivity. The landlord, commanding virtually unlimited labor, had little inclination to initiate improvements on his estate. The Indian had no particular desire to obtain agricultural education or to employ modern farm tools, for the acquisition of skill or implements would merely help to increase the landlord's profits. Lacking incentives for modernity and productivity, Bolivian agriculture failed to keep pace with the growing demands of an expanding population. Food that could have been produced within Bolivia had to be imported, a situation that threatened the country's sensitive balance of international trade. The cost of living soared steadily.

By the early 1930s, pressures, dislocations, and frustrations had reached a peak of intensity in Bolivia. The Chaco War ignited an open conflict that eventually culminated in revolution.

In 1932 Bolivia became involved in a border conflict with Paraguay. The territory in dispute was the Gran Chaco—on the face of it a wasteland of sorts. Bolivia's motivation for triggering the conflict was that the possession of the Gran Chaco would provide an outlet to the Atlantic through the waterways of the Río de la Plata system, a consideration of immense importance to landlocked Bolivia. Moreover, the Bolivians believed that the area contained rich petroleum deposits, a belief yet to be substantiated.

At the outset of the war, Bolivia appeared to be the superior power. Its population was three times that of Paraguay. Its army was larger, better equipped, and better trained. Assisted by German military advisers, the Bolivian general staff had forged a seemingly formidable army. (A German military mission had been established in Bolivia in 1911.)

These calculations collapsed under the fires of war. Raging between 1932 and 1935, the Chaco War spelled disaster for Bolivia. At the end, Paraguay assumed possession of most of the Gran Chaco, but Bolivia was promised an outlet to the sea. The loss of about sixty thousand men and the spread of disease throughout the country were some of the immediate consequences suffered by Bolivia. The undermining and eventual destruction of the military, political, economic, and social/psychological systems were among the long-term outcomes.

Prior to the Chaco War, the bulwark of Bolivian society had been the "invincible" army. As the war claims of glory faded, however, so also did the myth of invincibility. The war had exposed the Bolivian general staff as inept, incompetent, and incapable of leading effective military campaigns. Coupled with military ineptitude was a lack of human compassion. In the later stages of the war, conscripts were required to fill the thinking ranks of the Bolivian military. Most of the conscripts were Indians, who had to be forced to the front in chains, there only to confront inhuman conditions. "The front line of the Bolivian army was often a ragged mass of apathetic Indians, foully housed and fed; and, several miles in the rear, there was a second line of defense where 'gentlemen officers' lived comfortably, with ample food and drink, and often with the solace of their mistresses."[6] As the war drew to a close, the Bolivian army found itself discredited and demoralized.

Politically the war shook the foundations of the traditional regime and brought its legitimacy into question. The weaknesses of the old elite and the inadequacy of the feudal system were dramatically exposed. A cycle of coups and countercoups heightened tension and uncertainty.

A long and unvictorious war has more than military and political consequences. For one thing, a nation's economy is also affected. The Indian conscripts—some two hundred thousand in all[7]—had been taken from the mines and the land. The withdrawal of these laborers caused a drastic cutback in ore mining and food production. Under the pressure of new burdens, the already shaky Bolivian economy collapsed. The international balance of trade faltered as exports dropped and imports skyrocketed. Inflation soared, wiping out what little holdings the Bolivian people had managed to gather.[8]

As the military bulwark and the economic system crumbled, so did the social system. The war exposed white supremacy as a myth, opened up the Bolivian society to the Indians, and ended the Indians' isolation. The war experience provided the once immobile Indians with an inkling of political and social rights, privileges, and amenities. It acquainted them with the standard of living long enjoyed by the whites. In other words, it made relative deprivation a reality.

Having migrated to the cities and mining regions in pursuit of a better life, the Indians found themselves to be second-class citizens to whom avenues of progress were closed. Whereas in the prewar context such inequities would have been accepted as a matter of course, the new situation dictated a different response. The Indians demanded restitution for injustices previously suffered, a hearing on their grievances, and a higher standard of living.

The voices of protest, easily silenced before the war, found new outlets in the rubble the conflict created. Active discontent took root in the awakening second-class citizens, and among the intellectuals and university students as well. The faltering Bolivian Government was hard-pressed to control it.

The postwar atmosphere was highly conducive to the emergence of trade unions and political parties. Though organized labor was virtually destroyed during the war, postwar governments were generally sympathetic to the trade union movement, particularly in the mining industry.

The year 1936 saw the creation of Bolivia's first genuinely national labor organization, the Confederación Sindical de Trabajadores [Workers] de Bolivia. This was followed soon thereafter by the formation of the Federación Sindical de Trabajadores Mineros. The principal targets of the miners were the three "tin barons," Patiño, Hochschild, and Aramayo, who together dominated mining in Bolivia.

In the late 1930s and early 1940s Bolivia witnessed the rise of political parties committed to massive social change. Political parties—"liberal," "conservative," and "republican"—had previously operated in Bolivia, but they were all weak, all more or less status-quo oriented, and all more or less carbon copies of one another. By contrast, the new parties gave expression to a variety of demands and sought to remake the Bolivian society. Several parties vied for control and leadership of the emerging miner/peasant power base.

The Falange Socialista Boliviana (FSB) was established in 1936–37 by a group of Bolivian students in Santiago de Chile. The party was frankly patterned after Franco's Falange in Spain and took its name from that source. The students contented themselves with the publication of a manifesto and engaged in other propaganda activity. Lacking effective political leadership, the FSB languished as a political force.

The Falange was reactivated in the early 1940s as a result of the initial Nazi successes in World War II. It held its first congress in 1942 and made a heavy appeal to the discontented youth. Having fallen into disrepute after the defeat of the Axis, the party did not assume major importance in Bolivian politics until after the revolution of 1952.

Two of the major parties pursued a communist approach. The first of these was the Revolutionary Workers' Party (Partido Obrero Revolucionario, POR). Organized in 1940, the POR grew from an exiles' group, the Grupo Tupac Amaru, founded in Argentina during the Chaco War. The leaders of the party, including Gustavo Navarro (alias Tristán Maroff), were enthusiastic followers of Trotsky, and they soon affiliated with the Fourth International. Unified and cohesive, the POR has continued to be a major force in Bolivian political life.

The second communist-oriented party was the Party of the Revolutionary Left (Partido de la Izquierda Revolucionaria, PIR). Established in 1940, the PIR represented a merging of several small left-wing elements. It was proclaimed an "independent Marxist" party, led by and composed mainly of intellectuals. Foremost among the party's leaders was José Antonio Arze, a sociologist. In its early years, the PIR commanded great support in the leadership of the new labor movement. By 1943 it had turned this support into the control of Bolivia's central labor organization, the Confederación Sindical de Trabajadores de Bolivia.

The PIR was doing well in the late 1940s when a serious internal split developed. One wing of the party advocated close ties with the Soviet Union and subordination to Stalin's policies. The other wing pushed for an independent socialist program and policy. In 1950 the first group split to form the Communist Party. The PIR declined as a political force.

Between 1938 and 1942 a group of Bolivian intellectuals, in a series of meetings held in La Paz, debated various ideas dealing with the political situation in the country. The upshot of these meetings was the formation of another major party, the Nationalist Revolutionary Movement (Movimiento Nacionalista Revolucionario, MNR). (The exact date of the party's founding is a matter of controversy, although 1940 and 1941 are the dates most frequently given.) Among the founders were Víctor Paz Estenssoro and Hernán Siles Zuazo. The MNR was a nationalist party with socialist leanings, representing a coalition of many diverse elements, extending from the far right to the far left.

In the ensuing struggle for control of the Bolivian revolutionary movement, the strategy of the MNR proved viable and effective. Throughout the 1940s and early 1950s the party's leadership, ideology, organization, use of terror and violence, and manipulation of the international situation shaped and directed the political revolution in Bolivia.

LEADERSHIP

Where the revolutionary party is a coalition, as was the case with the MNR, the task of leadership becomes more arduous. Antagonistic factions of the party must be kept unified; competing perspectives and views must be harmonized. Hernán Siles Zuazo, Juan Lechín Oquendo, and Víctor Paz Estenssoro comprised the MNR's core of leadership and forged a cohesive organization from diverse factions and groups.

The spokesman for the moderate and conservative factions of the party was Hernán Siles. Born in La Paz in March 1914, Siles was the son of the former Bolivian president Hernando Siles (1926–30). Having graduated from the American Institute, a Methodist secondary school in La Paz, in 1931, Siles fought throughout the Chaco War and was decorated for bravery. At the war's end, he entered the University of San Andrés, also in La Paz, where he became active in leftist student politics and where he obtained a law degree in 1939. During the 1940s Siles served two terms in the Bolivian parliament (the Chamber of Deputies), where he distinguished himself as a man of courage and integrity.

A close friend of Paz Estenssoro, Siles played a key role in the formation and ascendancy of the MNR. Affluent, literate, and eligible to vote, Siles's supporters helped elevate the MNR to national prominence. Relying on them, Siles masterminded the pivotal election of 1951 (see below). Militarily, Siles was a skillful tactician. He was a central figure in the revolutionary fighting of both August 1949 and April 1952.

On the party's other extreme, Juan Lechín served as spokesman for the left. The son of a Lebanese merchant and a Bolivian mother, Lechín was born in 1914 in the mining town of Corocoro. Forced by poverty to leave school at age sixteen, Lechín became a driller in the Patiño mines. Having voluntarily fought in the Chaco War, Lechín returned to his home area, soon to become the country's most important labor leader. (Part of his early popularity is said to have been due to his consummate skill as a soccer player.) By 1944 Lechín had risen to head his local union. At about the same time, he helped establish the Federación Sindical de Trabajadores Mineros as a genuine national miners' union. He was elected executive secretary at the union's first congress in 1945.

Lacking political sophistication, Lechín in his early career depended on the advice of other union leaders, most of whom were affiliated with the Trotskyite POR. As a consequence, many of Lechín's policies and programs carried a communist flavor. Soon, however, several considerations propelled Lechín toward affiliation with the MNR.

To begin with, the POR lacked rank-and-file union support. Moreover, the union's identification with the POR invited a policy of suppression by the Bolivian government. Finally, Lechín had no particular ideological commitment to the POR; his actions "seem to have been motivated more by opportunism than by ideology."[9]

Lechín's disavowal of POR influence and his formal affiliation with the MNR vastly strengthened the latter. The MNR obtained the support of organized labor, broadened its political base, and gained in the person of Lechín a labor leader capable of solidifying the leftist factions.

While Siles consolidated the moderate/rightist factions and Lechín the leftist elements, neither group could alone hope for success. Only through a coalition of these diverse forces could a viable political organization emerge. In the person of Víctor Paz Estenssoro the factions found their common bond.

Paz was born in October 1907 in Tarija, southern Bolivia, of middle-class parents. Like Siles, he graduated from the American Institute and received a law degree from the University of San Andrés. Having fought and been decorated in the Chaco War, he returned to serve for a time as a lawyer in the Patiño company. Subsequently he functioned as a high-ranking officer in the ministry of finance and as a professor of economics at San Andrés. Paz was elected to the Chamber of Deputies in the late 1930s and early 1940s, at which time he also served as a founding member of the MNR. Shortly thereafter, Paz became MNR president, a position he held throughout the revolutionary movement, and beyond.

Moderate in outlook, Paz commanded the allegiance of both the right- and the left-wing leaders of the party. He maintained this allegiance by accurately judging the portent of events and then shifting position to accommodate them. The MNR's competing factions were willing to work together under Paz, for his opportunism helped bring the full power of the party to bear on issues of interest.

A sensitive and complex man, Paz Estenssoro was the pivotal link in a wide-ranging coalition and a main intellect behind revolutionary organization. Accompanying this

role as party leader was Paz's charismatic appeal to the
Bolivian people. He was capable of inspiring intense loyalty
and, at times, bitter hatred.

In summary, the leaders of the MNR were heterogene-
ous from a geographic, racial, and socioeconomic point of
view. They were born in different parts of the country,
represented a mixture of racial and cultural strains, and
came from the upper (Siles), middle (Paz), and lower
(Lechín) social strata. Beyond this, the MNR leaders constituted an indigenous, fairly homogeneous, relatively
young, and relatively well-educated group. They all served
in the Chaco War and played prominent roles in Bolivian
society and politics after the war. The chief characteristics
of the Bolivian leaders are summarized in Table 4.1.

TABLE 4.1

PROFILE OF BOLIVIAN LEADERS

Characteristic	Paz	Siles	Lechín
Date of birth	1907	1914	1914
Age in 1952	44	37	37
Place of birth	Tarija (southern Bolivia)	La Paz	Corocoro (mining town)
Social origin	Middle class	Upper class	Lower class
Occupation	Lawyer Professor Politician	Lawyer Politician	Miner Labor leader
Education	Law degree	Law degree	Some secondary
Foreign exposure	Moderate	Moderate	Small

IDEOLOGY

The ideology of the MNR has been a subject of considerable controversy. At one time or another, this ideology
has been characterized as communist, fascist, Nazi, and
Peronist.[10] Although a particular wing of the MNR did
espouse fascist and Nazi doctrines before the 1952 revolu-

tion, an examination of the program and actions of the MNR would reveal that the party's ideology was highly eclectic, with nationalist and socialist components.

The Program and Principles of Action of the MNR, adopted in 1942 and reaffirmed in 1946, embodied a number of interrelated objectives. The most important of these were: (1) national integration, extension of political and economic equality, and participation of workers and peasants in national life; (2) agrarian reform and the curtailment of the power of feudal elites; and (3) elimination of foreign economic influence and nationalization of the mines.

The Chaco War and its aftermath sensitized the MNR leaders to the deep fragmentation in Bolivian society and made national integration a prime objective. National integration involved nationalism, to be sure, but this nationalism, rather than being a reaction against colonialism or imperialism, sought to generate a broadly based sense of national identity and popular involvement in national institutions. The MNR quickly realized, however, that the desired integration was impossible unless the vast majority of the Bolivian population—the miners and the peasants—were drawn into national life and granted political and economic equality. To attain this objective, agrarian reform and nationalization of the mines were deemed necessary.

Fully conscious of the vast inequities fostered by the feudal system, the MNR sought agrarian reform. The party's 1942 platform put the matter directly and succinctly:

> We demand . . . that . . . every Bolivian, man or woman, [be made] a landholder. . . .
>
> We demand the identification of all Bolivians with the aspirations and necessities of the peasant, and we proclaim that social justice is inseparable from the redemption of the Indian for the economic liberation and sovereignty of the Bolivian people. . . .
>
> We demand the study on a scientific basis of the Indian agrarian problem so as to incorporate in the national life the millions of peasants now outside of

it, and to obtain an adequate organization of the agricultural economy so as to obtain the maximum
output.[11]

In the mid-1940s the MNR played an active role in call-
ing a National Indian Congress, at which the problems of
peasants were discussed by a range of participants including high government officials. The congress proposed a
series of reforms, including the abolition of the feudal system, but the full force of these reforms did not become
apparent until after 1952.

The goal of nationalization, particularly of the mines,
had no basis in communism, as has sometimes been
charged; rather, it was rooted in the conditions and needs
of Bolivia. The ideology of the MNR showed a bias against
economic imperialism and foreign business enterprises, but
such a bias was unavoidable in the Bolivia of the 1940s.

In the 1920s and 1930s, foreign capital, chiefly American, increased its stakes in Bolivia. In 1922, Standard Oil
of New Jersey acquired large oil concessions in southeast
Bolivia near the border of Argentina. In 1924, the United
States National Lead Company purchased a large interest
in the Patiño mines, the largest producer of tin in Bolivia.
Other companies obtained concessions in copper, lead, and
tungsten. Soon, foreign economic interests became dominant in Bolivia.

In the 1930s and 1940s, the products of mining industry constituted 90 to 95 per cent of the country's exports,
making the financial position of Bolivia heavily dependent
upon fluctuations in the world markets. And yet Bolivia
had little or no control over the mining industry. Economic
independence thus became a chief objective of MNR
ideology.

The nationalization of the Big Three mining enterprises,
which provided some 75 per cent of the country's total
mineral output, emerged as a necessary step toward a
measure of independence. For one thing, the Patiño,
Hochschild, and Aramayo mines were considered extensions of foreign capital. The three companies were substan-
tially owned by foreign enterprises: "about 28 per cent" of

the Patiño interests were owned by American concerns; Hochschild "was largely Chilean-owned"; and Aramayo "was financed by Swiss and British capital."[12] Moreover, as noted earlier, the "foreign tin barons" exported the wealth of the country to build vast fortunes abroad. Finally, the tin barons successfully used their economic power to influence governmental policy. The three companies "were waist-deep in politics and had long been hostile to the MNR. . . . They had subsidized candidates for office, they had financed revolution, they had made a regular policy of 'tipping' the local government officials in the mining areas."[13]

The MNR's strong nationalist stance brought forth charges of fascism, Nazism, Peronism, and anti-Semitism. Most of these charges were based on a misunderstanding or misinterpretation of the party's policies and objectives, and none of them made a necessary distinction between two important factions within the MNR.

From early in its history, there had existed within the MNR a split between a large moderate/leftist faction (as represented by Siles and Lechín, for example) and a small pro-fascist, pro-Nazi, pro-Perón faction (as represented by Carlos Montenegro and Augusto Céspedes, for example). Paz Estenssoro, rather than siding with either group, acted as mediator in an effort to prevent an open split within the party.

In January 1943 Paz, together with the rightist leaders but apparently without the knowledge of the leftist group,[14] formed an alliance with a military society known as Razón de Patria ("Cause of Fatherland," RADEPA). The RADEPA consisted of a group of young officers, all disillusioned veterans of the Chaco War, all profoundly influenced by fascism-Nazism-Peronism, and all anxious to rebuild Bolivia into a powerful nation.

The MNR-RADEPA coalition seized power in a coup in 1943 (see below). After the defeat of the Axis, however, the coalition government collapsed, the RADEPA fell into disrepute, and many MNR leaders (including Paz) went into exile in Argentina. There some of them came under the direct influence of Perón. This influence was temporary and uneven, and the MNR leaders gradually dissociated themselves from Peronism. The outright rejection of fascism-Nazism-Peronism did not take place, however, until after the revolution of 1952.

Paz Estenssoro was always sensitive to the charges of fascism-Nazism lodged by opposition parties and groups in an effort to discredit the MNR at home and abroad, particularly in the eyes of the United States. He stated in a speech in 1944:

> The principal objective of my speech is to demonstrate that the Movimiento Nacionalista Revolucionario is not Nazi, could not be Nazi. . . .
> We are the Revolutionary Nationalist Party. . . . We have seen that a country with a semicolonialist structure like Bolivia, in a revolutionary period, and within the present realities, must insofar as possible achieve a socialist regime which will permit the realization of social conquests appropriate to any nationalist policy, the grand objectives of which will be economic liberation and reform of the agrarian system. It is not possible to apply to Bolivia . . . principles applicable or already applied to other people in other countries. Here social phenomena are of a different nature. . . .
> . . . We profess a nationalism not of European extraction, even less one dependent on German nationalism. . . .[15]

In a May 1962 interview, Paz insisted on a fundamental distinction between the moderate/leftist/civilian wing of the MNR and its fanatical rightist/military counterpart. He denied that he had ever been close to Perón while in Argentina.[16]

Much has been written about the anti-Semitism of the MNR. The MNR's 1942 platform denounced dealings with foreign businessmen, particularly the Jews, as anti-national. The critics misinterpreted this policy as the establishment of a Nazi anti-Semitic line. The intent of the MNR program, however, was the liberation of the Bolivian people from oppression and exploitation by foreign business concerns. Dealings with foreign nationals were viewed as hindrances to the liberation of the Bolivian natives and to the creation of a unified Bolivian nation. The MNR policy mentioned the Jews by name because of their belated but forceful penetration of the Bolivian economy.

To enter the country, the Jews had bribed government officials. Having been admitted as agricultural immigrants, the Jews settled in the cities instead and opened businesses in competition with Bolivian merchants. According to one scholar, "a major scandal" of the Bolivian Government at this time "involved a cabinet minister who sold visas, at fees of $1,000 and more, to several thousand European Jews."[17] The MNR's anti-foreign policy rested not on the premise of a superior versus an inferior race but on the premise of an oppressed versus an oppressor group.

In summary, the MNR ideology was not Marxist, or communist, or fascist, or Nazi, or Peronist, or anti-Semitic. It was an eclectic and indigenous ideology, distinguished in its *lasting* features by nationalism, socialism, egalitarianism, and anti-feudalism—all geared to the peculiar conditions of Bolivia. As a response to popular desires and demands in the aftermath of the Chaco War, the MNR ideology set out to fashion a Bolivian nation, nationalize big business, terminate foreign economic exploitation, eliminate feudal agriculture, redistribute the land, support small capitalism and private property, construct schools, and expand the electorate. The appeal of the MNR ideology transcended classes and groups. The MNR leaders manipulated and diluted their ideology to pacify the opposition and gain support at home and abroad. They did not owe allegiance to any foreign power, nor did they fashion their ideology primarily to oppose one.

ORGANIZATION

The MNR, as we have seen, was primarily a political organization of the urban intellectuals. Effective leadership, ideological flexibility, and timely maneuvering enabled it to appeal to a wide spectrum of the Bolivian population, from the extreme left to the extreme right. A major source of MNR strength lay in its ability to capture the confidence and support of the emerging miner/peasant power base. Its organizational structure reached out to embrace not only the major urban centers but mining and agricultural regions as well.

By the mid-1940s, the MNR had evolved a centralized organizational apparatus. The final authority resided in the Party Leader (*Jefe*), who headed a National Command of about twenty-five members. All major policy making was centralized in this organ and in particular in its Political Committee of about half a dozen men headed by an Executive Secretary. This organizational structure was duplicated on the departmental level, so that each of Bolivia's eight departments had its own Departmental Command, Political Committee, and *Jefe*. Each Departmental Command performed a series of functions, including education, propaganda, mobilization, and the arming of the miners and peasants. In addition, each Departmental Command exercised control over a series of party cells that extended party organization into the local level.[18]

MNR organization went through distinct stages of development. In its early years the party concentrated on parliamentary politics. It sought to elect members to parliament and thereby gain access to cabinet posts where MNR leaders could place party policies in the national arena. Through this exposure, the MNR hoped to maximize popular support.

In 1940 the army engineered the election of General Enrique Peñaranda to the presidency. Although he had been an inept commander during the Chaco War, Peñaranda soon captured the influential support of the Patiño, Hochschild, and Aramayo elements by encouraging increased output in the tin industry.

In the election of 1942 the MNR, with the support of its moderate and conservative factions, elected Hernán Siles and one other party member to the Chamber of Deputies. This boosted MNR representation to five, three members having been chosen in previous elections.

At this point the MNR was unexpectedly thrust into national prominence. The Bolivian army, under orders from Peñaranda, put down the Catavi mine strike of December 1942, killing scores of men, women, and children in the process. The miners turned to the MNR for support. The MNR leaders in parliament took full advantage of the situation to blast the Peñaranda regime and champion the miners' cause. In so doing, they gained considerable popular support and expanded their power base in the labor movement.

Dismayed over its inability significantly to influence the course of events in Bolivia, the MNR adopted a new outlook. It departed from parliamentarianism to join forces with a military organization in order to seize governmental power. In January 1943 the MNR formed an alliance with the Razón de Patria. The RADEPA was a survivor of a secret military society, the Logia Militar Mariscal Santa Cruz, organized by Major Antonio Ponce in the bitterness and disenchantment of the post-Chaco era. The RADEPA continued to remain strongly pro-Nazi, pro-fascist, and pro-Peronist in ideology. It shared with the MNR a strong nationalist stance.

In December 1943 the MNR-RADEPA coalition overthrew the Peñaranda regime. In the new government, RADEPA leaders filled the top positions while the MNR assumed important cabinet posts. Major Gualberto Villarroel, of the RADEPA, assumed the presidency. Paz Estenssoro served as minister of finance.

From its newly acquired position of influence, the MNR set out to mobilize the miners and peasants. It encouraged and sponsored trade unionism, especially among the miners. It applauded the creation of the Federación Sindical de Trabajadores Mineros in 1944 and warmly greeted Juan Lechín's affiliation with the MNR. By the time of the revolution, the MNR dominated much of the labor movement and enjoyed solid rank-and-file support in the mine unions.

The MNR showed considerable concern for the peasants as well. In May 1945 it helped call the first National Indian Congress, attended by a range of participants including high government officials. The congress promulgated a decree abolishing the institution of compulsory personal service, defining the mutual obligations of landlords and tenants, and creating schools for peasants. Although these provisions were not seriously heeded by many landlords, the MNR had succeeded in mobilizing the peasants and in capturing their support.

Meanwhile, the Villarroel regime was confronting serious problems, and the MNR-RADEPA alliance began to waver. Viewing the new government as pro-Axis, the United States withheld recognition for six months and persuaded most other Latin American governments to do the same (see below). Unable to withstand the resultant diplomatic and economic pressures, President Villarroel dropped the MNR members from his cabinet and promised free elections. The United States extended recognition in June 1944, and new elections took place the following month. The MNR won an impressive victory and Paz Estenssoro and many other leaders returned to their posts in the Villarroel government.

After the defeat of the Axis, the RADEPA fell into disrepute. In order to reconsolidate his position, Villarroel again expelled the MNR members from their posts and organized an all-military cabinet. His rule was ended in July 1946, when a revolt broke out in La Paz in which the mob stormed the presidential palace.

The years 1946–52 were years of persecution and exile for the MNR. The Villarroel regime was followed by a civilian government headed by Tomás Monje Gutiérrez, a respected magistrate. In 1947 Enrique Hertzog, a La Paz physician and university professor, succeeded to the presidency. He soon turned the office over to his vice-president, Mamerto Urriolagoitia, who ruled de facto until 1951. The MNR had no representation in these governments. Many of its leaders, including Paz, went into exile. Many others were imprisoned. The most important leaders operating on a more or less continuing basis in Bolivia were Hernán Siles and Juan Lechín, though both of them, too, spent time in exile.

Under the Siles-Lechín leadership, the MNR underwent a new stage of organizational development and adopted a two-pronged program of political and military action. In general, it agitated, staged strikes, encouraged coups, and plotted against the government. Politically, the MNR ran candidates in every election between 1946 and 1952. It did surprisingly well, considering the restrictions placed upon it by the ruling regimes.

To complement its political activities, the MNR organized militarily. In the election of May 1949, the miners elected Juan Lechín as senator from Potosí. Within a month, the government, following a policy of firmness, arrested and exiled Lechín. The miners at Catavi immediately went on strike, cut off rail and communication lines, and seized some American engineers who worked in the mines. In the struggle that ensued, several dozen miners were killed and many more injured. Enraged, workers throughout the country went on sympathy strike. Eventually, however, the government regained control of the situation.

Three months later, in August 1949, the MNR engineered a series of unprecedented mass uprisings in the eastern, central, and southern parts of the country. No other organization had previously employed the Bolivian masses on such a scale, due to the common belief that the masses were apathetic and the common fear that mass involvement of Indians in an armed conflict might trigger an Indian insurrection. The MNR, however, had carefully cultivated the masses and was confident of their support. In particular, it had carefully armed the miners.

Leading the struggle was the team of Lechín (having returned from exile) and Siles. The MNR took control of several major cities through a series of rapid and coordinated attacks. After three weeks of fighting, however, the masses became increasingly frustrated, disenchanted, and impatient, and the uprising collapsed.

The principal focus of MNR political efforts in its exile years was the election of Paz to the presidency. In 1951 Paz and Siles formed a team to run for president and vice-president, respectively. Since Paz was in exile, the bulk of campaigning fell upon Siles. This was fortuitous, since most of the estimated two hundred thousand eligible voters in Bolivia at that time were from the middle and the upper classes.

Other pre-election events aided the Paz-Siles team as well. The government's forces were badly split in choosing a candidate. The leftist parties were fragmented and unable to put forward a unified program. Adding to these problems was a faltering, inflationary economy.

When the election results came in, Paz Estenssoro had captured a plurality amounting to 43 per cent of some 126,000 ballots cast. This was all the more impressive since suffrage was limited by literacy and property qualifications, the MNR had been denied access to implements necessary for running an effective political campaign (for example, its own press), and the presidential candidate was not even in the country. Paz claimed in an interview in 1956 that "the MNR . . . had discovered proof in government files that Paz had in fact received 79 per cent of the total vote" in the election of 1951.[19]

Since Paz had not received a clear majority, the actual selection of the president from among the top candidates was to be submitted to the parliament, as prescribed by the Bolivian constitution. At this point, a military junta headed by General Hugo Ballivián Rojas, commander of the La Paz garrison, took over in the name of "democracy" and in an effort to save the country from "an unholy alliance" of fascist, Nazi, and Communist elements.[20] The junta infuriated the public by voiding the election results, imposing martial law, issuing an anti-strike decree, prohibiting all public demonstrations, and controlling the press.

The junta's behavior sparked the second major military action of the MNR. For a year, the party organized, mobilized, armed the workers, and prepared to seize governmental power. In particular, it created a Revolutionary Committee to assume over-all direction of the struggle. The party established the "Groups of Honor" (Los Grupos de Honor), paramilitary units consisting of five hundred to eight hundred men responsible for co-ordinating the military efforts of the MNR in La Paz and elsewhere.[21]

The major lesson learned from the 1949 failure was

that, to seize power, the revolutionaries must capture the key cities quickly and decisively. And so, on April 9, 1952, the MNR, under the leadership of Lechín and Siles, attacked La Paz with a force of about one thousand men. The action proved highly effective and the fighting ended in the afternoon of April 11. Simultaneous attacks had been launched in the major cities.

An event of major importance that took place a few days before the actual fighting was the defection to the MNR of General Antonio Seleme, minister of government in the Ballavián Cabinet and chief of the national military police. Seleme's defection was motivated by a personal ambition to become president, but he panicked and took refuge in the Chilean embassy in the afternoon of April 9, when he thought the revolution was about to fail. Seleme's defection brought the revolutionaries much needed moral and material support, including a trained force of about three thousand military police and a rich supply of arms and equipment.

Acting as provisional president, Siles proclaimed the election of 1951 as the foundation of the MNR government. Paz Estenssoro returned from exile on April 15 to assume the presidency.

TERROR AND VIOLENCE

Throughout its history, Bolivia had been a country governed by terror and violence, which were widely considered "reasonable and accepted alternatives" to political activity.[22] Governmental resort to terror and violence was a characteristic means of maintaining the status quo; opposition resort to terror and violence, a characteristic means of challenging it. The transfer of political power almost routinely involved the use of force.

Physical and psychological violence were regularly visited upon the workers and the peasants. The peasant's life, as we have seen, was a perpetual condition of coercion and force. The worker did not fare much better: strikes, demonstrations, and other expressions of dissatisfaction were vigorously put down by the political authorities.

In this context, the MNR must be considered rather unusual in shying away from the *routine* employment of terror and violence. When in power, the party did imprison or exile its opponents, but it did not undertake wholesale violence against the Bolivian population.

Alberto Ostria Gutiérrez, minister of foreign affairs under Peñaranda, has provided us with a detailed account of the exercise of terror and violence in the Bolivia of the 1940s.[23] The Villarroel government (1943–46) did indeed torture, abuse, persecute, imprison, and murder its political opponents, but as Robert J. Alexander has pointed out, Ostria "does not present any direct evidence to link the MNR" with these activities.[24]

When the MNR-RADEPA coalition fell from power, the ensuing governments adopted a policy of systematically suppressing, isolating, and weakening the MNR. Top party leaders were exiled. Hundreds of lesser figures were imprisoned. Throughout the MNR's years of exile, governmental reliance on force was quite pervasive.

Governmental terror and violence extended to union leaders as well as to the rank-and-file members who supported the MNR. In 1947, for example, the Patiño mines discharged all their laborers. Rehiring was then carried out by accepting only workers who were non-union and not affiliated with the MNR. These policies ignited a strike against which the government sent troops. In suppressing the strike, the army killed two union leaders and dissolved the union as an organization.

When the MNR returned to power in 1952, terror and violence were used to neutralize the forces of the opposition. On the whole, however, the MNR leaders showed a fairly sophisticated understanding of the advantages and drawbacks of a policy of reliance on force. Throughout the prerevolutionary period the MNR continued to organize, with the full knowledge that such activity would provoke governmental response. Governmental terror as a reaction to MNR activities mobilized the Bolivian people toward the party's program. In the words of Ostria, organization, rather than terror, provoked the government "into taking harsh and not always strictly legitimate measures of self-defense, which had the effect of generating sympathy" for the MNR.[25]

Alexander has argued persuasively that the principal reason for the MNR's reluctance to undertake massive terror and violence was that the MNR was "a well-organized and well-disciplined political party which knew from the beginning what it wanted to achieve and more or less how it wanted to achieve it. This party had a history going back more than a decade before the beginning of the . . . Revolution, had had previous experience in exercising governmental power, had known the bitterness of persecution and exile, and had built up a wide mass following."[26] The MNR did not hesitate to use extensive violence when the situation demanded it, however, as in 1949 and 1952.

THE INTERNATIONAL SITUATION

In the MNR leaders' attempt to seek international aid for themselves and neutralize support for the opposition, relations with two countries deserve special attention: Argentina and the United States.

Bolivia's powerful neighbor to the south was of serious consequence, because Perón was in a position to offer the revolutionaries both material assistance and physical sanctuary. The MNR leaders, through their alliance with the RADEPA, had established rapport—and in some cases close acquaintance—with Perón. This friendship enabled the revolutionary leaders to take sanctuary in Argentina. Perón was helpful even to the point of providing employment for some of the exiled leaders.

It is worth reiterating that Paz Estenssoro, himself in exile in Argentina for a time, insisted in a May 1962 interview that he was never close to Perón. In fact, he claimed, he was driven from Argentina to spend his last two years of exile in Uruguay.[27]

Relations with Perón cooled as the revolution appeared

to have bogged down, but after Paz's victory in 1951, Perón once again extended assistance to the exiles. Some have claimed that the success of the 1952 revolution owed much to Perón, but these claims remain unsubstantiated.

In their relationships with the United States the Bolivian revolutionaries walked a diplomatic tightrope. U.S. attitude toward the MNR shifted radically over the years. Having held the MNR members of the Villarroel regime (1943–46) responsible for the pro-Axis orientation of that government, the United States withheld recognition for six months until the MNR leaders were expelled from their posts. Indeed, through the promulgation of the Guani Doctrine (December 24, 1943), the United States discouraged the other American states from recognizing new governments in Latin America without prior consultation with the U.S. State Department.[28] Argentina and Ecuador were the only countries openly to challenge the doctrine, and Argentina the only country actually to recognize the Villarroel government. After the U.S. declaration of war on the Axis powers, American FBI agents helped create in Bolivia a "National Bureau of Investigation . . . to combat undercover Nazi-Fascist activity."[29]

During the MNR's years of exile, the United States continued its hostility toward the MNR leaders on the ground that they had become the ideological allies of Perón. Following the revolution of 1952, the U. S. Government described the MNR as "Marxist rather than Communist" and launched a program of economic assistance to prevent a communist take-over.[30] The United States came to realize that the MNR was not in fact fascist, Nazi, or Communist and set out to maintain cordial relations with its leaders.

This change of U.S. attitude was due in no small part to the activities of the MNR leaders. The MNR attitude toward the United States has in fact alternated among skepticism, friendship, and at times hostility. The MNR leaders were fully aware of the U.S. policy of sustained intervention in the internal affairs of Latin American states. Moreover, in the intellectual climate of the Bolivia of the 1930s and 1940s, anti-imperialism and anti-

Americanism were quite fashionable positions. Lenin's theory of imperialism, according to which the advanced, capitalist societies would inevitably subordinate and exploit the smaller, underdeveloped countries, held wide currency among Latin American intellectuals. Nevertheless, in order to bring about the United States' neutrality toward the revolutionaries—and possibly to capture positive assistance—the MNR leaders frequently adopted ideological positions compatible with its international stance.

In the early 1940s Paz Estenssoro made a number of statements designed to lay the groundwork for cordial relations with the United States. He declared in 1943, for example, that the MNR had co-operated with the RADEPA in overthrowing the Peñaranda regime because that regime "had not co-operated closely enough with the United States." He added: "In the future, we shall continue to support the United Nations [that is, the Allies]. All international commitments, as well as the Atlantic Charter, will be scrupulously respected by the new government."[31]

In a speech a year later, Paz denied that the MNR had ever used "the international situation to improve our political position," because this would invite "the intervention of foreign powers . . . and subordination of the sovereignty of Bolivia." However, he went on to add, "With the United States joining one side of the present war, we, a country economically dependent, producing raw materials and needing manufactured goods, in our own interest could not and cannot be against the United States." He reiterated the point that Bolivia would "align itself with the United Nations, and cooperate with them in the development of their war program."[32]

During its years of exile, the MNR attempted in various ways to undermine American support for the Bolivian regime. For example, the MNR leaders "tried to sabotage United States-Bolivian relations by making contact at Montevideo with Assistant Secretary of State Edward J. Miller, then on a tour of Latin America, and presenting him with a memorandum to the effect that 'any economic or financial assistance that the Bolivian government might obtain would be wastefully spent and would not be of lasting benefit.' "[33]

During and after the 1952 revolution, the MNR continued a policy of friendship toward the United States and the international community at large. Although the MNR leaders had previously looked with disfavor upon a 1951 United Nations mission in Bolivia (on the grounds that it violated Bolivia's sovereignty), they now adopted an accommodating attitude toward the mission and applauded its assistance. The MNR's ideology of establishing a unified Bolivian nation, expanding the electorate, and protecting private property had always appealed to the United States. The MNR gained further legitimacy in U.S. eyes by its participation in parliamentary politics and in particular by the convincing Paz-Siles victory of 1951. Upon his assumption of the presidency, Paz welcomed American aid and assured the American tin interests that he would not interrupt their Bolivian supply. He succeeded in convincing the United States that the nationalist/leftist MNR was far more desirable than the groups with which it competed.

SUMMARY

The Bolivian Revolution was the culmination of a series of military, political, economic, and social/psychological changes set in motion or aggravated by the Chaco War. Too fragile to withstand the massive frustration and discontent the war created, the social structure burst open in what the white dominant class dreaded most: mass political action by the repressed groups.

The leaders of the Bolivian Revolution came from diverse socioeconomic and racial backgrounds; they were indigenous, well educated, and relatively young. The ideology of the revolution was indigenous and eclectic, with heavy nationalist and socialist components. In seeking national unity, extension of political and economic equality, agrarian reform, nationalization of the mines, and curtailment of the power of traditional elites, the revolutionary ideology captured widespread popular support.

As a revolutionary organization, the MNR had solid bases of support in urban centers, mining areas, and agricultural regions. Careful ideological maneuvering enabled the party to appeal to important segments of the Bolivian population. MNR organization underwent distinct stages of development. In the late 1930s and early 1940s, the MNR concentrated almost exclusively on parliamentary politics. In 1943 it turned to military action to capture political power, an effort that was a qualified success. From 1946 on, it combined political and military activity in a concerted effort to remake the structure of Bolivia's society, economy, and polity. Throughout, the MNR paid careful attention to organizing and mobilizing the miners and the peasants and, in particular, to arming the former.

The MNR adopted a conscious policy of shying away from the indiscriminate use of terror and violence. The party did imprison or exile its political opponents but it did not undertake wholesale violence against the Bolivian population. A principal reason for this policy was that the MNR was a well-established political party enjoying considerable public confidence.

The MNR leaders were well aware of the international implications of a possible revolution in Bolivia. In an effort to undermine the opposition and capture support for itself, the MNR diluted its ideology and took stances complimentary to those of the United States and Argentina. It succeeded in convincing the United States that the MNR offered the most viable political alternative for Bolivia.

Chapter 5

NATIONAL REVOLUTION: NORTH VIETNAM

The desire for national independence and the concomitant hatred of the outsider were the most important dynamics molding the Vietminh Revolution. Vietnam was a unified and centralized country by 1802. With the French colonial wars of 1858–83 Vietnam lost its name, unity, and independence. It was known for approximately eighty years as Tonkin (the North), Annam (the Center) and Cochin China (the South). Throughout this period, an incipient nationalism gathered momentum and finally burst forth in the 1940s. The alternatives of the Vietnamese people were relatively clear during the Vietminh assertion of control: to follow nationalist albeit Communist leaders or to remain under French colonial rule.

CONDITIONS

A vast array of preconditions—economic, psychological, social, political—coalesced to set the stage for the Vietminh Revolution. The major economic difficulties revolved around the French tax and land policies. Taxation was based more on French fiscal needs than on the native population's ability to contribute. The French had monopolies on alcohol, salt, opium, and tobacco; the taxes on these products provided a significant portion of the colony's revenues.

The salt tax is illustrative of French fiscal policies. In the period 1897–1907, the taxes imposed on salt catapulted its price fivefold. In the same period, personal income and local taxes for the natives doubled in Tonkin.[1] The French themselves paid almost no taxes. The universal head tax was a small matter to the comparatively wealthy French settler, but it could be ruinous to the peasant.

The French land policies were as poorly conceived as their tax programs. The output required of the peasants drove them into debt or into renting land they had previously owned. The rent and the interest on loans were so high as to force thousands of debt-ridden peasants off their land. There arose, as a result, a large landless class, oppressed by and alienated from society.

As the condition of the peasantry deteriorated, the gap between expectation and achievement created frustration throughout the countryside. The situation was no better in the urban centers, where the educated native elite was confronted with a persistent discrepancy between aspiration and actuality. John T. McAlister, Jr., has applied to Vietnam Ted Gurr's theoretical model of relative deprivation as the basic condition of civil violence. He identifies a group of relatively well-educated Vietnamese whose socioeconomic advance was thwarted by inadequate employment opportunities. He focuses on a second group of native intelligentsia who had achieved a degree of socioeconomic advance but no corresponding political power. Introducing a political variable into Gurr's psychoeconomic model, McAlister maintains that the denial of political power to the intelligentsia—and the resultant discrepancy between socioeconomic status and political influence—was a most important source of discontent leading to revolution. He believes that much of the impetus for the Vietminh Revolution came from the relatively small segment of the Vietnamese population that had experienced some social mobility in the colonial context, but no commensurate political power.[2]

French colonialism was phenomenally inefficient and unresponsive in Vietnam. The oft-promised tax and land reforms never materialized. Monopolies continued to flourish. In some seventy years of colonial rule, the French constructed dozens of prisons but only one university. Only a fraction of Vietnamese children got even an elementary education. In 1943 the colonial government spent five times as much on opium (to be distributed through French monopoly) as on education, libraries, and hospitals combined.[3]

Early attempts to create a University of Hanoi and a native high school system met with strong opposition from the French settlers, chiefly because education heightened the political consciousness of the natives. Such measures as were taken—for example, sending bright Vietnamese students to France—were too little and too late. The victory of Japan over Russia taught the Vietnamese that Western knowledge was a most important weapon for defeating the Western powers. As a result, many natives left for Japan, underground study groups and newspapers began to appear, and traveling lecturers began to stress the importance of an educated native elite. All this activity was spurred by the realization that education had been denied as a means of suppression.

Some of the reasons for French callousness and unresponsiveness are all too clear: the repressive aims of French colonialism, the profit motive of the French settlers, the fear of an educated indigenous elite, the uniform ineptitude of governors general due to political patronage in Paris.

Revolutions occur, in part, when large segments of an oppressed population anticipate relief through open defiance of the existing regime and an appeal to an alternative one. Such an awareness probably did not become widespread in Vietnam until the Japanese occupation of World War II. The comparative ease with which the Japanese subjugated the French exploded the myth of French military invincibility. During this period, various nationalist groups merged into the League for the Independence of Viet Nam, founded by Ho Chi Minh in 1941 (see below). Thus emerged the possibility of a viable indigenous alternative to French colonialism.

When Ho Chi Minh proclaimed Vietnamese independence on September 2, 1945, and Bao Dai (the puppet emperor installed by the departing Japanese) abdicated in Ho's favor, support for the Vietminh regime became synonymous with the defense of the country's new-found freedom. There was no viable non-Communist alternative, and a return to colonial subjugation was unthinkable. This was crystallization of developments that had been slowly taking shape for decades. The French, however, re-established control, banned the Communist Party, and forced Ho to continue the struggle for national independence.

LEADERSHIP[4]

The dramatis personae of the Vietminh Revolution include Ho Chi Minh, Vo Nguyên Giap, Pham Van Dong, Truong Chinh, and Le Duan.

A charismatic leader and superb organizer, Ho was born in 1890 in the village of Kim-Lien in Nghe-An province of central Vietnam. Ho's grandfather earned the equivalent of a Master of Arts degree and was appointed a district governor, a post from which he was dismissed for insubordination. Ho's father, also the recipient of a higher degree, refused to accept a mandarin post and joined a dissident intellectual group instead. Arrested and imprisoned in 1907, he was placed under permanent house arrest following his release in 1910. Thereafter, he earned a meager living as a practitioner of Chinese medicine.

Ho Chi Minh attended a French lycée at Vinh but was expelled at the age of thirteen for anti-French activities. Having earned a lower degree in 1907, he was appointed an elementary school teacher, a job he soon deserted to participate in nationalist activity.

From 1911 to 1913 Ho served as a mess boy on a French liner, traveling extensively in Europe, Africa, and America. This experience profoundly embittered Ho by providing him with firsthand knowledge of the oppression and exploitation practiced by the Western powers in colonial areas. The humiliation Ho experienced in his dealings with the Europeans personalized the colonial struggle for him.

In 1913 Ho settled in London for a few years, where he worked as a kitchen helper and shoveled snow for the

London school system. He moved to France in 1917 and came under the heavy spell of French socialism and communism. Having joined the French Socialist Party, he attended the 1920 party congress that approved the formation of the French Communist Party. In 1922 he traveled to Moscow as a party delegate to the fourth congress of the Communist International. He returned to that city in 1923 and again in 1924 and remained there to study communism.

In 1925 Ho accompanied Mikhail Borodin to China, ostensibly to work as a Chinese translator at the Soviet consulate in Canton but in reality to operate as a Comintern agent in Indochina. While in Canton, Ho founded the Vietnam Revolutionary Youth League (Viet-Nam Thanh Nien Cach Menh Dong Chi Hoi). This organization was in fact a training school in Marxism-Leninism; later, Ho's students dispersed to introduce communism throughout Vietnam.

In 1930 Ho founded the Indochinese Communist Party (ICP). At about the same time, he was appointed head of the Far Eastern division of the Comintern, which activity precluded his effective leadership of the Communist movement in Vietnam. Ho's whereabouts throughout the 1930s remain something of a mystery. He reappeared on the scene in 1941, however, to devote his entire attention to problems of communism in Vietnam. From a small political party, Ho forged an organization that eventually controlled North Vietnam, influenced the South Vietnamese, Laotian, and Cambodian Communists, and drove the French out of Indochina.

Admirer of Napoleon, personification of the evolving doctrine of people's war, and victor of Dien Bien Phu, Vo Nguyên Giap was the military mastermind of the Vietminh Revolution and the individual most responsible for forging a full-fledged modern army from a guerrilla band of thirty-four men.[5] Giap was born in 1912 in the village of An-Xa in Quang-Binh Province of central Vietnam (immediately adjacent to Ho's birthplace of Nghe-An), one of the poorest areas. Giap's father, though poor, commanded much respect as a scholar and intellectual. An ardent nationalist, he regularly participated in anti-French activities.

In 1925 Giap was sent to a French lycée, where he organized and led a series of student demonstrations. Arrested and sentenced to three years' imprisonment, he was soon released for good behavior. Having determined to concentrate on his studies, Giap received from the University of Hanoi an LL.B. in 1937 and a doctorate of laws (highest degree awarded) in 1938. Meanwhile he taught history at a private school in Hanoi, where he succeeded in influencing many of his colleagues with his revolutionary ideas.

Giap joined the ICP in the mid-1930s. His wife, also a revolutionary, was arrested in 1939 (following the outlawing of the ICP by the French) and sentenced to life imprisonment; she died in prison in 1943. Giap's bitterness peaked when his sister was arrested and guillotined.

When he met Ho Chi Minh, in South China in 1941, Giap had already acquired a reputation as a Communist leader. Charged by Ho with the task of organizing the Vietminh armed forces, Giap soon forged an effective military apparatus capable of staging small operations against the French. By 1946, when the revolution got fully under way, Giap's forces were quite capable of launching major military campaigns.

Relatively little is known about many of the high-ranking Vietminh leaders, including Pham Van Dong, Truong Chinh, and Le Duan. Pham Van Dong was born in 1906 in Quang Ngai (Cochin China) to an aristocratic family. His father was a scholar at the court of Hué and held the post of cabinet chief. An intense nationalist, Pham Van Dong is credited with a long history of revolutionary activity. Having entered the University of Hanoi in pursuit of a baccalaureate in 1925, he immediately took a leading role in a series of student strikes and demonstrations. Threatened with arrest, he fled to China, where he met Ho Chi Minh and joined the Vietnamese émigré group in Canton. Pham Van Dong soon returned to Hanoi on a po-

litical mission, where he was arrested and imprisoned in
1929. Upon his release, he resumed his revolutionary activities in Hanoi and Saigon until 1939, when communism
was outlawed. Having fled to China with Giap, he participated in the formation of the Vietminh in 1941 (see
below).

Truong Chinh, the foremost intellectual and chief theo-
retician of the Vietminh Revolution, was born around
1908. A founding member of the ICP, he was active in
revolution throughout the 1930s and the 1940s. He was
appointed secretary-general of the Communist Party, a position he held for over a decade.

Truong Chinh is an admirer of the Chinese and at times
has followed their example slavishly. A prime illustration
is the very name "Truong Chinh," an alias meaning "long
march" in Vietnamese. Another is Truong Chinh's sponsor-
ship of a brutal and catastrophic agrarian reform program
in 1954–56, presumably patterned after the Chinese, which
led to his downfall and public self-criticism.

Le Duan was born in 1907, of peasant origin, in a small
village in the province of Quang Tri, central Vietnam.
Little is known of his childhood and youth. In 1929, Le
Duan was recruited by Ho Chi Minh into the Vietnam
Revolutionary Youth League. A year later, he became
a founding member of the ICP and the top Communist
leader in Annam. In 1936, after spending five years in
prison for anti-French activities, Le Duan went to Hué,
a center of revolutionary ferment, where he remained
until 1939. Having outlawed the ICP, the French again
arrested and imprisoned Le Duan for another six years.
Released in 1945, Le Duan went to Hanoi to become a
high-ranking Communist official and eventually to replace
Truong Chinh as secretary-general of the party. A key
party bureaucrat and operative, Le Duan has conducted
his activities under a general cover of mystery.

In summary, the Vietminh leaders were nationalist before they were Communist or Marxist. Most of them came
from rural areas and many from a background of anti-
French, nationalist, revolutionary activity. They were, as
a rule, fairly young and fairly well educated. Ho Chi

Minh, though widely traveled, received less formal education than most and was in his fifties when the revolution unfolded. The Vietminh leaders were generally of middle-class origin and had experienced some upward socio-economic mobility in the colonial system. The main characteristics of the revolutionary leaders are summarized in Table 5.1.

IDEOLOGY

The most important component of the Vietminh ideology was nationalism. The leadership was Communist and Marxist, to be sure, but its objective as well as that of the masses was first and foremost national autonomy and the elimination of French colonial rule. "Nationalism," Joseph Buttinger has written, "was an integral part of the Vietnamese Communist cause, not merely a cover for their real aims."[6]

To the Communist revolutionaries, Vietnam appeared a living laboratory of Lenin's theory of imperialism, according to which the Western capitalist countries would inevitably and persistently exploit and oppress the underdeveloped countries of the East. Communist propaganda untiringly condemned the French for their continued enslavement of the peoples of Indochina, stressed the brotherhood of all peoples and their common cause against imperialism, projected the Communists as ceaseless fighters for national independence and people's welfare, and emphasized the army's love for the people and the people's love for the army.

Much of the struggle was based on Mao Tse-tung's theory of protracted conflict, in which the guerrilla is of the people as the fish is of the sea.[7] A protracted struggle, from the standpoint of the revolutionaries, undergoes three stages of development: strategic defensive, strategic stalemate, and strategic counteroffensive. The revolutionaries being weak, Mao had taught, they were bound to lose ground in the initial phase of the conflict. In the meantime, it was necessary to develop a war of maneuver over

TABLE 5.1
PROFILE OF VIETMINH LEADERS

Characteristic	Ho Chi Minh	Vo Nguyen Giap	Pham Van Dong	Truong Chinh	Le Duan
Date of birth	1890	1912	1906	1908	1907
Age in 1946	56	34	40	38	39
Place of birth	Cent. Vietnam (rural)	Cent. Vietnam (rural)	So. Vietnam	?	Cent. Vietnam (rural)
Social origin	Middle class	Middle class	Middle class	?	Middle class
Occupation	Teacher Menial worker Comintern agent	Teacher	Teacher Journalist	?	?
Education	Elementary	Doctor of Laws	College	Tech. schl.	?
Foreign exposure	Extensive	Moderate	Moderate	Moderate	?

a vast territory to harass the enemy and undermine his effectiveness and morale. This required mass political mobilization, a united front of the "whole people," and the development of peasant guerrilla warfare on a national scale. Having attained sufficient strength, the revolutionaries would then launch a counteroffensive to destroy the enemy.

By the mid-1930s the Communist ideology was widespread, albeit thinly, throughout Indochina. As the Soviet model of communism, with its emphasis upon the proletariat, was inappropriate for Vietnam, the Vietnamese Communists increasingly gravitated toward the teachings of Mao Tse-tung. Attempts were made to infiltrate local governments and to form secret underground organizations where recruitment, training, and propaganda proceeded ceaselessly.

With the outlawing of the Indochinese Communist Party at the outbreak of World War II, many Vietnamese Communists fled to China. In May 1941 Ho Chi Minh called a congress in Kwangsi Province attended by former members of the ICP and by other left-wing and nationalist groups. The conference resulted in the formation of the League for the Independence of Vietnam (Viet-Nam Doc Lap Dong Minh Hoi), thereafter commonly known as the Vietminh. Although from the start the Vietminh was led and dominated by the Communists, its declared primary objective was the freedom of Vietnam. Communist ideology was played down, because the leaders were in Nationalist China and because they hoped for Chinese as well as American aid. Ho Chi Minh and his associates were determined, however, that the Vietminh would follow a Communist doctrine.

On August 7, 1945, the day after the bombing of Hiroshima, Ho Chi Minh announced the formation of the Vietnam People's Liberation Committee as his provisional government. Giap's guerrillas, now some five thousand strong, on that day assumed the title of the Vietnam Liberation Army. Ho and Giap had patterned their forces on the Chinese experience as described in Mao Tse-tung's writings on guerrilla warfare. This experience emphasized the need for internal political cohesion and solidarity, mobilizing and organizing the masses, and establishing and equipping secure base areas. Mao's Three Main Rules of Discipline and Eight Points for Attention became guidelines in all military activity.[8] The Vietminh forces were taught to observe strict discipline in their activities, extend fair treatment to the local people, protect their property, be concerned with their welfare, and help them in their daily work. A vast propaganda network was organized throughout the country. With some exceptions (see below), the exercise of force was limited to eliminating anti-Communist or anti-Vietminh officials, especially if they were locally unpopular.

With the abrupt surrender of the Japanese, the Vietminh quickly infiltrated Haiphong, Hanoi, and many other areas in the North in order to claim the powers of government. The Vietminh apparatus worked exceedingly well, and by the end of August 1945 Ho Chi Minh was in control of all Tonkin and northern Annam except for Hanoi and Haiphong. Ho's victories generated a vast groundswell of nationalist feeling, of which the Vietminh, with characteristic speed, took full advantage. Stimulated by Vietminh agents, village committees sprang into existence all over the North. The committees took over local administration and in some cases adopted harsh methods in liquidating the former officials. In the South, Communist commander Tran Van Giau assumed control of the United Party (a coalition of nationalist and Communist forces) and quickly gained control of a large section of Cochin China.

On August 29, 1945, Ho Chi Minh dissolved the People's Liberation Committee and announced the formation of a Provisional Government of the Democratic Republic of Vietnam. A few days later, on September 2, he proclaimed the existence of an independent Democratic Republic of Vietnam and severed all ties with France. It remained for him to come to an agreement with Giau in the South.

Meanwhile the Potsdam Conference had assigned to (Nationalist) China control over northern Vietnam, and to the British control over the South, the dividing line being the sixteenth parallel. In a series of bloody battles, the French, with the active support of the British, re-established control in Cochin China and gradually extended their grip to the North. Ho Chi Minh had no alternative but to continue the struggle until 1954.

Throughout the struggle, the Vietminh made a conscious effort to dilute the Communist ideology in order to attract nationalist and leftist groups. In 1945, Ho Chi Minh voluntarily disbanded the Indochinese Communist Party in a gesture of devotion to the nationalist cause, and he made every effort to propagate the slogan "Fatherland Above All." The reappearance in 1951 of communism in the form of the Vietnam Workers' Party (see below) is itself testimony to Vietminh sensitivity to avoid the term "Communist" in order to maximize public support. The Declaration of Independence of the Democratic Republic of Vietnam (September 2, 1945), drafted by Ho Chi Minh himself, appeals to and quotes approvingly from the American Declaration of Independence and the French Declaration of the Rights of Man and Citizen.[9] Finally, the Vietminh made a habit of giving the nationalists a number of seats in the National Assembly and other high councils of state, a practice that was continued for some time even after the capture of power in 1954.

ORGANIZATION

The chief objectives of Vietminh organization were to facilitate political control and to develop an effective military apparatus. An impressive array of political organizations played a key role in spreading propaganda and generating mass mobilization from the earliest days of the Communist movement.[10] As early as June 1925, while in Canton, Ho Chi Minh founded the Vietnam Revolutionary Youth League, an organization of political exiles. Having carefully indoctrinated the members of the League in the Communist ideology, he dispersed them to organize Communist cells in Vietnam.

From 1925 to 1930 a series of parties, clubs, and study

groups were formed in Vietnam, of which the most important were the New Vietnam Revolutionary Party
(1926) and the Vietnam Nationalist Party (1927). The
ineffectiveness of these and similar organizations was due
in part to their localist orientation and in part to fragmented leadership. Meanwhile the French authorities
spared no effort in arresting party leaders and outlawing
political organizations.

In 1930 Ho founded the Indochinese Communist Party.
Consisting preponderantly of Vietnamese, together with
small representations from Laos and Cambodia, the party
dwindled for lack of effective leadership. Ho's absence from
Indochina throughout the 1930s precluded meaningful su-
pervision and control of party affairs. Having been outlawed by the French in 1939, the ICP went underground.

In May 1941, Ho organized the League for the Independence of Vietnam (the Vietminh). An amalgam of
nationalist, leftist, Marxist, and Communist elements, the
League received much impetus from the Japanese invasion
of the country. It was the only organization to rise above
parochialism and fragmentation and emerge as a full-
fledged national force.

The Vietminh penetration of Vietnamese society was
greatly facilitated by the fact that, having been asked to
perform intelligence and other functions for the Allies
(particularly the United States and Nationalist China)
early in World War II, the Vietminh forces received all
necessary co-operation, supplies, and equipment from the
Americans and the Chinese. The Japanese occupation
weakened the French, strengthened the Vietminh, and permitted the latter to establish an intricate organizational network, complete with bases, throughout the country.

In November 1945, the Indochinese Communist Party
dissolved itself to permit the formation of the Vietnam
People's Front (Lien Viet) as a means of resisting the
French reoccupation of the country. In fact, however,
the Communist Party continued its clandestine existence
for another five years, during which time it increased its
numbers and influence throughout Vietnam.

In February 1951 Ho Chi Minh announced the formation of the Vietnam Workers' Party (Viet-Nam Lao Dong Dang), which has continued to be the ruling regime in Hanoi. Though the new party represented the first overt reappearance of communism since the Indochinese Communist Party, two contrasts in the very names are suggestive: "Vietnam" (rather than Indochina) indicates an increasing self-awareness and self-confidence, and "Workers" (rather than Communist) represents a concession to the more moderate forces and an attempt to unite all factions and groups.

The Vietminh military doctrine closely followed the pattern established by Mao Tse-tung.[11] Giap and his associates turned to serious study and application of the works of Mao after a series of defeats at the hands of the French in the winter of 1946–47, when the Vietminh troops attempted to give an account of themselves in set-piece battles. The core of Mao's teachings in this regard was a protracted struggle based on peasant guerrilla warfare beginning in the countryside and closing in on the cities. Base areas were to be chosen with great care, after due attention was given to the ruggedness of the terrain, sympathy of the local population, and the availability of food and supplies.

Although primary attention was devoted to guerrilla and mobile warfare, the decisive character of positional warfare in crippling the enemy never escaped Giap, by nature a less patient man than Mao Tse-tung. Despite the lesson of 1946–47, Giap was to attempt positional warfare on a large scale on two other occasions: in 1951, with disastrous results for the Vietminh, and in 1954, with shattering effects on the French.

The Vietminh military was from the start subject to strict political control and centralized authority; the political officers were the most influential elements in the military structure. By the end of the 1940s, the Vietminh tightly controlled an imposing military apparatus and actively pursued Communist objectives consistent with nationalist goals. The relatively simple military organization of the early 1940s gradually evolved into a complex apparatus consisting of three subdivisions: the Political Bureau, the General Directorate of Supplies and Maintenance, and the High Command.[12]

The Political Bureau integrated the military and political objectives of the Vietminh. In the early years of the war, when the co-operation of the non-Communist elements was considered essential, the power of the political officers in the military was limited. As the Vietminh gained power in the government, the authority of the field officers increased as well; eventually they came to hold veto power over decisions made by their military counterparts. In addition to the regular political apparatus within the military, a secret party organization merged with the political apparatus on various levels to intensify discipline and control.

The General Directorate of Supplies and Maintenance played a crucial role in Vietminh victory, particularly, as we shall see, at Dien Bien Phu. The Directorate had several sections variously concerned with food, clothing, medicine, transportation, supply, ammunition, and repair. The Directorate became increasingly centralized as the Vietminh military became complex, but it continued to maintain a high level of effectiveness.

The High Command was reorganized several times during the struggle. Its chief functions included personnel, intelligence, communications, planning, and operations. Directly under the High Command came the Vietminh forces, which were divided into three groups of varying combat capabilities: the regular army, the regional forces, and the popular troops. Well trained and equipped, the regulars' basic function was to wage a war of maneuver on their own initiative as to timing, location, and terrain. The regional forces supplied the regular troops, protected their retreat and advance, launched small attacks, harassed the enemy, and helped train the popular forces.

The popular troops consisted of two groups: The Dan Quan was composed of persons of all ages who performed auxiliary military duties by collecting intelligence, engaging in sabotage, serving as guards, acting as porters, repairing roads, and building fortifications. The Du Kich was made up of men between eighteen and forty-five who, as part-time guerrillas, concentrated on harassing and confusing the enemy. The great political and psychological value of the two groups was that they created an impression of a national struggle in which the entire population took part.

The Vietminh military operations were masterminded by Giap, and their effectiveness rested on several interrelated factors. All military activity was based on Mao Tse-tung's dictum that "The enemy advances, we retreat; the enemy camps, we harass; the enemy tires, we attack; the enemy retreats, we pursue."[13] Several specific principles guided Vietminh behavior on the battlefield. The first of these was maintaining the initiative. The time, place, and conditions for each battle would be selected with great care and after careful consideration of the condition of the enemy. This required a sophisticated intelligence system, which the Vietminh commanded with great skill and to which we shall return momentarily.

The second principle was speed of movement. Forces would concentrate rapidly, take position quickly, strike decisively, and disappear instantaneously. Marching at night, the Vietminh would develop a position without alerting the enemy. The attack would take place at dawn. The assault and the retreat would be executed with maximum speed. The Vietminh were seldom caught without a plan of retreat.

Another principle was surprise. Without deception and cunning, the Vietminh agreed with Mao, it would be impossible to fight a superior enemy. Surprise included striking at the enemy when and where he least expected, harassing in one place and attacking in another, leading the enemy on and encouraging overconfidence, and attacking in the dark. A favorite device was to leak inaccurate information to the enemy in order to mislead him into an ambush; to this end, fake documents were planted on double agents, for example.

A further principle was undermining enemy morale. Communist agents would infiltrate French camps to encourage treason and spread propaganda. Threats of violence and terror were made against pro-French elements

(see below), and on occasion bribes were offered for co-
operation.

Finally, the Vietminh would attack only if victory was
certain, that is, if the manpower ratio was decisively in
their favor, or if, through surprise or ruse, they had gained
a clear advantage over the enemy. This involved an efficient intelligence system, which the alien French could not
command.

The Vietminh intelligence apparatus was quite elaborate.
Intelligence has two aspects: maintaining secrecy about
oneself and capturing maximum information about the enemy. The Vietminh enforced strict security measures and
prohibited their officers and men from discussing military
matters outside official meetings. "Careless talk" was forbidden. Troop movements were carried out at night, and
the main routes were avoided.

Vietminh agents were scattered throughout the country
to infiltrate French positions and gather information on
French movements. According to one writer, "The Vietminh intelligence service had penetrated right into the inner
recesses of the various headquarters. This robbed the
French of any element of surprise. . . . The Vietminh
were always one jump ahead, no matter how hard they
[the French] schemed, how secretive they were, or how
cunningly they planned."[14]

The Quan Bao, or Military Intelligence, was composed
of party members especially chosen for physical, mental,
and moral qualifications and given special training. On occasion these agents used comparatively modern methods
(for example, radio intercept) to obtain information; more
characteristically, they relied on direct interrogation of both
the local civilians and enemy personnel—a task at which
they excelled. For example, they would interview prisoners
of war several times for long periods and at hours when
the prisoners' resistance was lowest. They would display
sarcasm toward the prisoners, hoping to generate anger
and impatience, in the course of which the prisoners would
reveal more than they intended. Agents were slipped into
prisoners' cells to pose as other prisoners.

The Vietminh usually attacked at night because the

French were considered inferior night fighters and because their air and artillery support was less effective in the dark. To overwhelm the enemy, the main effort was character-istically concentrated on a very narrow front, while smaller units created diversions. The Vietminh would attack from various directions in order to increase the psychological pressures on the enemy, who had to face constantly shifting battle lines. The French forces rested under the dreaded possibility—which often materialized—of waking up sur-rounded.

The Vietminh were particularly adept in laying ambushes for enemy forces. The chief objectives of ambush were to inflict casualties, capture arms and ammunition, block supply or relief routes, obtain information, divert and dis-perse enemy forces, and harass and demoralize the enemy. Certain conditions were deemed essential to the success of an ambush: full intelligence about the enemy, favorable terrain (including ease of access from several directions), sufficient manpower, co-ordination of the attack, speed of action, surprise and diversion, and rapid withdrawal. As an enemy column approached, it met a Vietminh force block-ing the road. As the column halted, it was met with fire not only from this group but also from two others located on either side of the road and one to the rear of the column.

The battle of Dien Bien Phu was a most atypical opera-tion in the Vietminh Revolution and totally at variance with the strategy of protracted struggle.[15] It was a classic nineteenth-century battle with a surrounded defense posi-tion sustaining constant attacks from artillery and land forces. The French decided to defend Dien Bien Phu be-cause it could be used to block Vietminh movements in and out of Laos and because it had two airstrips and served as intersection of three roads. The French com-mander, General Henri Navarre, believed, moreover, that Giap could not divert the number of men necessary to take the fortress and that any positional warfare would hurt the Vietminh more than the French.

Surrounded by heavily wooded hills, Dien Bien Phu is set in a flat paddy-field basin measuring about twelve miles in length and eight miles across. It was located about 170 air miles from the French air bases in Hanoi, a considerable distance for effective support and supply. The Vietminh began settling into the surrounding hills in January, and the French patrols were gradually restricted in their movements.

Giap's plan for Dien Bien Phu called for an initial round of attacks on March 13, to be followed by a second round on March 30, a period of encroachment, and a final series of assaults. The initial attacks were intended to take the three outlying French positions at Beatrice, Gabrielle, and Anne-Marie and to facilitate assault on the stronger, central positions. Isabelle, to the south, was to be dealt with later.

By the middle of March, Giap had four divisions of regulars in the hills surrounding Dien Bien Phu. He placed his heavy guns singly along the fringe of hills to the east. Manned by the Chinese Communists, anti-aircraft guns were also dispersed singly.

On March 10, the Vietminh guns shelled the airstrip that served as the only means of French movement and supply. The French Air Force retaliated by dropping napalm and bombs on the assumed positions of the enemy guns, but Vietminh camouflage effectively masked their exact locations.

The initial series of attacks enabled the Vietminh to capture the three northern French positions by the night of March 17–18. French morale remained high, however, because of the large number of enemy dead (around 2,500) and because the French still maintained that they could beat the elusive Vietminh in a slugging match. They were jolted, nonetheless, by the intensity and accuracy of Vietminh firepower. Moreover, the enemy anti-aircraft gunners had destroyed or badly damaged twelve French aircraft in three days. The airstrip was, by the fifteenth, out of action, being too riddled to accommodate landings and supplies. The second airstrip, at Isabelle, was useless, as the Vietminh had largely isolated that position. From this point on, French reinforcements and supplies had to be parachuted in, an exceedingly hazardous operation.

Psychological pressures mounted as Giap began to close

in by digging a huge trench around Dien Bien Phu, within a mile of the French defenses. Meanwhile, the Vietminh had completed a motor road extending from Lai Chau (near China, in the northeast) to within ten miles of Dien Bien Phu, thus dramatically improving their supplies. Endless coolie columns were now supplemented by Russian Molotova trucks. The arrival of a complete anti-aircraft regiment was particularly welcomed. The guns, manned entirely by Chinese Communists, posed a deadly problem for all French aircraft.

A few days before the end of March, Vietminh fire died down, leading the French into believing that the Communists, like themselves, were running low on ammunition. The ruse worked well, as the French did not expect the sudden all-out attacks on their main positions on March 30. The assault lasted until April 4, as the French defenses proved tougher than Giap had anticipated. He tried to break into the center of the perimeter by way of the northeast and the northwest but was effectively blocked. The familiar pattern of mass attacks on a narrow front had not been quite sufficient.

The third phase of the siege (the period of encroachment) lasted from April 5 until May 1. The Vietminh troops closed in simply by digging from the encircling trench toward the French. At this time the Vietminh forces were nearly fifty thousand strong, while the fortress had only about sixteen thousand defenders. The Vietminh supplies were far superior to the French. Moreover, they captured much of the matériel dropped on Dien Bien Phu by French aircraft and intended for the defenders.

The final series of assaults began on the evening of May 1. On May 2 the Communists were fairly well beaten back, and for the next three days the Vietminh infantry put in assault after assault on all sides. Slowly the French perimeter began to buckle. One by one the positions and outposts were overrun as the fire of the defenders was blocked by the sheer number of Vietminh dead draped over the barbed wire. On May 7 the Vietminh broke through into the heart of the defenses, and the battle ended that evening. Isabelle, to the south, fell on the next day. The French had suffered more than seven thousand casualties and the Vietminh about twenty-three thousand.

The battle of Dien Bien Phu was fought consistent with Giap's conviction that a decisive engagement may shorten a protracted struggle. Having been wary of protracted sieges since a series of defeats at the hands of the French in 1951, Giap gradually concluded that a successful general offensive involving positional warfare would facilitate the taking of Hanoi and would deliver a political, psychological, and military blow sufficiently crippling to be felt in Paris and thus shorten the war.

The Geneva negotiations began shortly after the fall of Dien Bien Phu. Giap and his troops had given the Vietminh negotiators a much stronger political and psychological posture vis-à-vis the French.

TERROR AND VIOLENCE

In the 1940s the Vietminh organized a security system throughout the country as a means of collecting taxes, recruiting men, increasing the number of informers, conducting intelligence, collecting rice, and eliminating opposition forces and officials. Especially heavy taxes were imposed on suspected French supporters and sympathizers—itself a form of terror, since it created anxiety and deprived hostile elements of a portion of their livelihood.

The Communists began to eliminate many nationalist leaders—potential competitors for power—after World War II and just prior to the outbreak of hostilities with the French in December 1946. During the first weeks of the struggle many nationalists were killed after sentencing by "people's courts." Public "trials" of ranking citizens and native officials, "criticism and self-criticism," and other implements of Communist purge were extensively employed.

In the late 1940s and early 1950s, the Vietminh assassinated or in other ways disposed of many village officials associated with the French pacification programs. They made examples of individuals in order to frighten any natives tempted to co-operate with the French.

In 1953 the Communist authorities launched a wave of terror in the North ostensibly as a reaction against non-payment of taxes. Actually, the Communists had a list of "traitors" whose guilt they sought to prove by forcing the villagers to name them as ones who allegedly had advised the people to withhold taxes. The names "confessed" by the villagers were frequently supplied by their torturers, and the people soon discovered that the beatings stopped when they mentioned the appropriate names. Later Ho Chi Minh went on the air to apologize for the failure of his leadership in permitting the "masses" (actually Communist agents) to take the law into their own hands and ignore the Party's and the government's good intentions. By then, of course, the Vietminh had obtained the "proof" needed against the "traitors."

The more typical modes of torture included compelling the victim to kneel down while supporting on his head a basket full of rocks, hanging the victim by the feet and either beating or jerking him about, wrapping the victim's thumb in oil-soaked rags and then igniting them. Usually the party disclaimed any guilt, and known party members left the scene when atrocities occurred.

The Vietminh also used terror to highlight the vulner-ability of both the French troops and the French residents in Vietnam. Communist suicide squads would attack French posts in both urban and rural areas, and would conduct sabotage operations against the French. When selecting targets for sabotage, the Vietminh were careful to con-sider possible consequences of their actions for the local population. No target would be sabotaged near a friendly village, for example, lest retribution fall on the inhabitants. By contrast, the Vietminh would post snipers near hostile or indifferent villages being approached by French troops. These snipers would pick off several of the forward elements and then disappear. The French, upon arrival, would blame the villagers for the shooting and would kill many of the inhabitants. As a result, some formerly hostile vil-lages were neutralized while some formerly neutral villages were driven into the Vietminh camp.

The Vietminh ceaselessly sought to subvert the non-

French members of the French force, such as the Legionnaires, the North Africans, or the Vietnamese. One of the chief methods was the distribution of pamphlets urging desertion and promising good treatment. The Vietminh would also use blackmail (for example, threats of reprisals against families) in order to encourage desertion.

In the North the Vietminh generally used terror to advantage; with some exceptions, they did not employ terror haphazardly or indiscriminately. The situation was different in the South, where the Vietminh commander, General Tran Van Giau, seemed convinced that unity demanded the summary elimination of anyone who refused blind allegiance. He persecuted nationalists, Trotskyites, religious leaders, and any other group that put up the least resistance. Communist terror in the South under Giau and later under his replacement Nguyên Binh became counterproductive and drove many neutral elements into the French camp.

For their part, the French did all in their power to stem the tide of nationalism and communism by violent means. They banned political parties and labor unions, summarily executed their opponents as a means of setting examples, imprisoned political leaders and violently dispersed their followers. They maintained concentration camps throughout the country, the best known being Poulo Condore. The slightest resistance to French policies was suppressed with crushing force.

At times, French terrorist activity became unimaginably brutal. Joseph Buttinger has described the year 1931, for example, as "a year of White Terror" in Vietnam. One estimate, Buttinger writes, put "the number of victims at 10,000 killed and 50,000 deported. There is no darker year in the history of French rule in Vietnam than 1931. People were killed not in the heat of battle—there were no battles—but rather they were chased, hunted down, and murdered by a soldiery drunk on blood." These policies "evoked indignation, shock, and shame" not only in Vietnam but in France as well.[16]

Similarly throughout the 1940s and early 1950s the French responded to Vietminh guerrilla activity by intensifying their indiscriminate policy of terror in both the cities and the countryside. French terrorism propelled large segments of the population, even those formerly friendly to France, to identify with the Vietminh.

THE INTERNATIONAL SITUATION

International factors proved crucial at several points in the Vietminh Revolution. Throughout, the Vietminh demonstrated an acute sensitivity to the world situation and a determination to exploit it to advantage.

The Japanese occupation of the country during World War II not only weakened France but also indirectly enhanced the position of the Vietminh. Throughout the occupation, the Americans, the Chinese, and the French relied on the Vietminh to harass the Japanese and gather intelligence on enemy movements. In particular, the American OSS (Office of Strategic Services) established direct contact with the Vietminh. In order to enable the Vietminh to perform the functions assigned them, weapons, supplies, and equipment were provided.

As noted earlier, the Vietminh toward the end of the war had dissolved the Indochinese Communist Party in order to court the favor of Chiang Kai-shek's Nationalists and to dissuade the Americans from aiding the French colonialists in their expected reassertion of control. Attempts were numerous, during the early years of the Vietminh resistance, to soft-pedal the Communist ideology and the Communist character of the Vietminh leadership in order to maximize public support, avoid alienating non-Communist powers, and deny the French rationalization for fresh intervention in Vietnam. As suggested earlier, the Declaration of Vietnamese Independence appealed to the principles of the American Declaration of Independence and the French Declaration of the Rights of Man and Citizen. These were in effect attempts to minimize or neutralize foreign opposition and court the favor of potential allies.

During the Nationalist Chinese occupation of Vietnam (following the Japanese surrender), Ho was careful to include many non-Communists in his provisional government in order to appease Chiang Kai-shek. Several nationalist parties and groups held offices in Ho's government, though they were later weeded out.

The victory of the Communists in China in 1949 brought the Vietminh both material support and international respectability. Mao's regime immediately launched a far-reaching program of military and technical assistance to Vietnam. Chinese technicians and experts, foodstuff and supplies, arms and ammunition began a steady flow into Vietminh territories. Most important, perhaps, the Chinese provided the Vietminh with a safe rear guard. Several Communist camps, located inside China, were beyond the reach of the French and immune to French air attacks.

International respectability ensued when China recognized the Democratic Republic of Vietnam (DRV) on January 18, 1950, the first country to do so. The Soviet Union followed suit on January 30, and was in turn followed by Poland, Rumania, Hungary, and North Korea. The DRV was also informally recognized by the delegations represented at the Bandung conference of April 1955. Indonesia, India, and Pakistan began formal relations with the DRV soon after the conference.

As the revolution intensified, the DRV became increasingly dependent for weapons, ammunition, trucks, and supplies on the Soviet bloc and Communist China. However, most weapons and matériel used by the Vietminh were captured from foreign sources. For example, in a series of defeats inflicted upon the French in the fall of 1950 alone, the Vietminh captured "13 artillery pieces and 125 mortars, 450 trucks and three armored platoons, 940 machine guns, 1200 submachine guns, and more than 8,000 rifles."[17] After 1950, the Vietminh gained access to American military equipment and supplies through the Chinese Communists, who had captured them from Chiang's troops. More significantly, after the settlement of the Korean conflict in 1953, much of the captured American military hardware was directed to Vietnam. As a result, at times Vietminh weapons turned out to be more modern than those of the French.

The Vietminh received support and sympathy from

forces within France herself. The French Communist Party established ties with the Vietnamese Communists and sought to hinder the French war effort. "It was estimated at times that up to 40 per cent of some of the consignments of military equipment were sabotaged before they reached Indochina."[18] This was naturally aggravating and demoralizing to the patriotic French fighting in the jungles of Vietnam.

At the conclusion of the Korean negotiations, in July 1953, the Vietnamese Communists, with the assistance of the French Communist Party, spread rumor abroad of impending negotiations between the French and the Vietminh. This included the point that the French had approached the Vietminh but that, in a show of confidence and strength, the Vietminh had turned them down.[19]

The Soviets and the Chinese were influential in persuading the Vietminh to accept the provisions of the Geneva accords. The two Communist countries were apprehensive that continued fighting in Vietnam might lead to a much wider international conflict. The United States by this time was voicing hope and support for a non-Communist South. Ho Chi Minh, probably fearful of jeopardizing relations with the USSR and China, settled for the possession of Tonkin and northern Annam (the area north of the 17th parallel) and the promise of future unification of Vietnam.

SUMMARY

The Vietminh Revolution fed on widespread frustration and discontent generated by French colonial policies. The disparity between expectation and achievement among both the educated strata and the masses of the people was a fundamental condition of revolution. The denial of political influence to the native intelligentsia created potential revolutionary leaders. French callousness to the needs of the Vietnamese people provided the Vietminh with much of their following.

Relatively young, fairly well educated, and coming from a rural middle class, most Vietminh leaders had amassed

considerable nationalist and revolutionary experience before the onslaught of the final struggle with France. Nationalist above all, the Vietminh leaders employed the
Marxist-Leninist ideology as a means of driving the French
out of Vietnam. Marxism-Leninism effectively addressed itself to the conditions of Vietnam and blended smoothly
with Vietnamese nationalism. Lenin's theory of imperialism
found ready acceptance among the exploited Vietnamese.
Throughout the struggle, the Vietminh made a concerted
effort to dilute the Communist ideology in order to attract
support at home and abroad.

Beginning with meager resources, the Vietminh leaders
forged a political/military apparatus eventually capable of
confronting the infinitely superior forces of the French.
They constructed a vast propaganda network in an effort
to improve communication and intelligence, mobilize and
politicize the masses, and draw the people into revolutionary
action. They relied upon Mao Tse-tung's conception of
protracted struggle based on peasant guerrilla warfare. The
battle of Dien Bien Phu, though atypical of military operations in Vietnam, was fought consistent with Giap's perception that a decisive engagement, if successful, would
generate a sufficiently powerful political and psychological
momentum to force the French out of the country.

Both governmental terror and revolutionary terror were
used extensively throughout the Vietminh Revolution. The
French relied on terror and violence—at times indiscriminately—to stem the tide of nationalism and communism, a
policy that helped turn the population against them. The
Vietminh relied upon terror and violence in order to eliminate opposition groups, stress the vulnerability of French
forces, and demoralize the enemy. On some occasions, they
employed violence indiscriminately.

The Vietminh leaders demonstrated an acute sensitivity
to the international situation and the importance of capturing foreign allies and international assistance. On numerous
occasions, they soft-pedaled the Communist ideology in order to attract potential support. They received crucial material and spiritual assistance from the Chinese.

Chapter 6

ABORTIVE REVOLUTION: FRANCE, 1968

The French Revolution of 1968 underwent three stages of development: (1) May 3–13: beginning at the Sorbonne, a student protest movement rapidly picked up momentum to envelop the French academic community; (2) May 13–30: spreading to factories and professions, the protest became a full-scale political movement; (3) May 30–June 30: the movement began a denouement culminating in President Charles de Gaulle's decisive victory at the polls.

On the afternoon of Friday, May 3, 1968, about five hundred leftist students gathered in the central courtyard of the Sorbonne to protest the closing of the Nanterre Faculty of Letters, and especially to demonstrate their objection to the summons issued to six Nanterre *enragés* ordering them to appear the following Monday before the university's disciplinary council for allegedly harassing students and insulting staff. Used originally in a derogatory sense to describe an extremist revolutionary group of the 1790s, the term *enragés* was applied to the Nanterre militants by Gaullist authorities and proudly embraced by the students. The new *enragés* were unsparing critics of their community who sought to use the university as a springboard for political revolution.

The rector of the Sorbonne, Jean Roche, and the minister of education, Alain Peyrefitte, apparently alarmed at the sight of five hundred students—some armed with legs of broken chairs and other makeshift weapons—made the fateful decision to call in the police. The police, arriving in their black vans—long-hated symbols of repression—surrounded the students and cordoned them off into small groups, forcing them into the vans. Other students looking on became outraged at the sight of their comrades being packed into the vans. "All hell broke loose when the first police vans left the Sorbonne."[1]

As was to be the case throughout the ensuing weeks, police action served to perpetuate violence rather than stifle it. The mere presence of the police mobilized and united the students as never before. The invasion of the university by the police—an open violation of an ancient tradition—together with indiscriminate exercise of police force captured unprecedented public support for the students. Even such an embittered critic of the May revolution as Raymond Aron was forced to write: "For weeks on end, Parisian opinion, as if in the grip of some ideological debauchery, seemed to be unanimous in its worship of 'admirable youth.'"[2] Within hours the movement spread to the entire university community in Paris, and the student leaders called for a demonstration for Monday, May 6. The spontaneity with which events unfolded was to be a prominent characteristic of the French Revolution of 1968.

Though officially banned, the demonstration turned out to be massive. "On Monday," said *Le Monde* of Wednesday, May 8, "Paris saw its most impressive and threatening demonstration for many years. Even during the Algerian War there had never been a movement of such breadth and above all such staying power."[3] Begun in a peaceful fashion, the demonstration turned violent as the participants clashed with the police through the night.

During the week of May 6, the student insurrection engulfed Paris and spread rapidly to the provinces. Barricades sprang up throughout the Latin Quarter as students sought to neutralize the advantages of the police. Liberal professors and intellectuals declared their sympathy with the students. Schoolboys in many lycées went on sympathy strike. In a pivotal meeting on the night of May 9, representatives of a number of leftist groups from Belgium, Italy, the Netherlands, West Germany, and elsewhere declared their solidarity with their French comrades and called for the transformation of the student movement into a general struggle of the working class.

On several occasions the students reiterated their demands: the granting of amnesty to the arrested students, the withdrawal of police from the Latin Quarter, and the reopening of the Sorbonne. Meanwhile the government of Charles de Gaulle combined characteristic intransigence with uncharacteristic inaction. As if paralyzed, the regime seemed unable to evolve a policy responsive to the situation at hand. The police cordoned off the Latin Quarter, and government spokesmen from time to time attributed the entire difficulty to the work of foreign elements, anarchists, nihilists, and Trotskyites.

The night of May 10–11—since romantically dubbed "The Night of the Barricades"—served as a transition from the first to the second stage of the revolution. In a large demonstration on the afternoon of May 10, the students reiterated their demands and asked for a share in the running of the universities. Receiving no satisfaction, they decided to capture the Latin Quarter by force. They split up into small groups to frustrate the launching of a single, directed attack by the police. They tore up paving stones, their ubiquitous and favorite weapon, readily available from the roadway and easily loosened by a screwdriver. Using the stones, overturned cars, street signs, and assorted debris, the students set up dozens of barricades.

Shortly before 2 A.M. the police charged the first barricades. Heavy fighting ensued for four hours as the police, in charge after charge, drove the students from their defenses. At about 5:30 A.M. the students reluctantly dispersed, having lost many comrades to prisons but with their morale unshaken.

On the following morning, Saturday, May 11, Premier Georges Pompidou returned from a diplomatic trip abroad. Taking immediate command of the situation, the Premier, in a televised address that evening, reaffirmed his faith in the youth of the country and announced the release of the arrested students, the withdrawal of troops from the Latin Quarter, and the reopening of the Sorbonne. Pompidou's action dismayed and demoralized the authorities, especially the police, who interpreted his action as a disavowal of their policies. A strike by the police unions was narrowly averted.⁴ "Unconditional surrender," wrote Raymond Aron.⁵

But the Premier was too late. On that morning, for reasons to be discussed below, France's most powerful labor unions, together with their academic counterparts, called upon their members to go on a twenty-four-hour general strike and demonstrate on the following Monday, May 13, the tenth anniversary of de Gaulle's presidency.

The Monday demonstration brought out some eight hundred thousand persons. It was a triumphant march and a massive demonstration of student/worker unity. The student revolutionaries drove home the point that they were no longer the *groupuscules* (tiny groups) that the critics pejoratively labeled them. In retrospect, the leaders of the revolution considered the mass intervention of the working class their greatest achievement.

Following the demonstration, the students headed for the Sorbonne, which Premier Pompidou, true to his promise, had ordered reopened. Having occupied the Sorbonne, the revolutionaries set up a "student commune" that lasted for over a month. There they tested some of their ideas about self-management and direct democracy and engaged in endless discussion and debate. They created a general assembly, an executive committee, and a series of subcommittees to handle food, lodging, health care, press relations, and other services. Not insignificantly, they found it necessary to create a *"Service d'Ordre."* In lighter moments, they engaged in theatrics and a bit of self-mockery. They wore theatrical costumes captured at the Odéon Theater; they covered the walls of the Sorbonne with such slogans as "Take the Revolution seriously, not yourselves." On June 16, the government used a knifing incident as a rationale to end the Sorbonne occupation, with relatively little resistance from the students.

Meanwhile the twenty-four-hour general strike of May 13 had mushroomed into a wave of spontaneous factory strikes spearheaded by younger workers in defiance of the unions. Bypassing the union leadership and using the Sorbonne occupation as a model, militant workers occupied and ran their own factories all over France. "Workers' so-

viets" and "workers' control" became universal slogans.
Within ten days, an estimated eight to ten million French
workers (about half of France's entire labor force) had
become involved in the strike.

The upheaval was no longer a localized university protest. It affected all areas of France and all strata of the
population. Its objective was the overthrow of the Gaullist
regime and the restructuring of French society. Revolutionary fervor reached lawyers and physicians, journalists
and newscasters, scientists and engineers, churchmen and
librarians, artists and musicians, painters and writers, high
school students and their teachers.[6] The revolutionaries
created "Action Committees" to mobilize the masses and
draw them into the struggle.

Breaking his silence on May 19, President de Gaulle declared at the end of a meeting of the ministers: "La ré-
forme, oui; la chienlit [bed-messing], non!" In a nationwide address on May 24, he called for a new mandate
through a new referendum. Outraged by the general's un-
timely arrogance (the Conseil d'État—France's highest court
—declared the referendum unconstitutional), the revolutionaries called for a demonstration on the evening of May
24 that resulted in extensive street fighting and the burning
of the Paris Bourse (stock exchange). The struggle picked
up such momentum, the revolutionaries thought in retrospect, that they could have brought down the Gaullist regime had they only proceeded to capture ministries and
other public buildings.[7]

During the period of May 25–27, the Gaullist regime
conducted uninterrupted negotiations with the labor unions.
The result, an agreement announced by Premier Pompidou
on May 27, represented major government concessions on
wages, fringe benefits, and working conditions. While the
union leaders immediately accepted the agreement, the
workers flatly rejected it, reaffirming the latter's belief that
the strikes had more than economic motivation.

On May 29, President de Gaulle left Paris in secrecy to
fly to Baden-Baden to consult with the commanders of some
seventy thousand French troops stationed in Germany. Re-
crossing the border to Mulhouse, near the Rhine, he fur-

ther consulted with key French military officials, who assured him of the army's loyalty to the Fifth Republic. This assurance was not without conditions, however, as de Gaulle promised to release General Raoul Salan and other right-wing political prisoners of the Algerian War.

De Gaulle's three-minute speech of May 30 signaled the third phase of the French Revolution of 1968. Speaking at 4:30 P.M., the General announced that he would fulfill his popular mandate by fighting for the life of the Fifth Republic. He announced the dissolution of the National Assembly and the holding of new elections in June. The country was in the grip of "totalitarian communism," he said, and he would do all in his power to avert such a take-over.

The last statement was inaccurate, but the ploy worked effectively. By 6 P.M., hundreds of thousands of persons flooded the Champs-Élysées for three hours to chant the *Marseillaise* and demonstrate unprecedented support for the Gaullist regime. "Most collars in the crowd were clean; medals were worn; many of the women wore gloves and were of an age to remember de Gaulle's triumphant progress down that splendid avenue at the Liberation."[8] Critics charged that the Gaullist authorities had made careful preparations for the demonstration, including prior distribution to the participants of special gasoline rations, by then an extremely scarce commodity.[9]

Within days the entire atmosphere had been transformed. The May revolution literally collapsed. By mid-June most of the strikes had ended, though some factories continued to hold out. On June 12 the government banned all demonstrations and declared illegal a dozen activist organizations. In the elections of June 23 and June 30, the Gaullists won an overwhelming victory, increasing their parliamentary majority by nearly one hundred seats.

CONDITIONS

France in the 1960s experienced some of the same conditions prevalent in other prerevolutionary societies. Economic, social, political, and psychological signs of discontent were evident throughout France.

Although France had had a relatively prosperous economy throughout the decade, in at least one respect the economic situation was analogous to what it had been in 1789, when, as Crane Brinton noted, "prosperity was certainly most unevenly shared."[10] Similarly in the 1960s, as one writer has found, "the top 10% of the [French] population earn[ed] over seventy-five times more than the lowest tenth."[11]

Probably the most economically disgruntled element in France is the factory worker. He works nearly forty-eight hours per week, the most among the Common Market countries. He earns less than his counterparts in those countries, with the exception of Italy. Also, purchasing power declined more sharply in France in the 1960s than in any other Common Market country.

The gap between the workers' income and that of the middle and upper income groups sharply widened. A nationwide fear of mass unemployment reached an intensity unknown in postwar France. The workers received no effective help from the unions, because, where unions existed and were recognized (only about 25 per cent of France's twenty million workers are unionized), they suffered from unresponsiveness, overbureaucratization, and paternalism. The worker felt exploited by and separated from society. He had no share in the making of decisions that affected his daily life and no recourse by way of appeal. He experienced a pervasive feeling of thwarted aspiration.

Operating under great constraints, the French educational system was on the verge of collapse. The French student population nearly tripled during the regime of Charles de Gaulle, and state expenditures on education rose correspondingly. (The University of Paris alone boasted a student body of 130,000.) Overcrowding, impersonalization, centralization, authoritarianism, and outdated curriculums created frustration and discontent. A favorite banner slogan captured the mood of the students: "Look at us and what do you see? A can of sardines!"[12]

Some 70 per cent of French university students dropped

out without obtaining degrees, and, among those who did finish, a large proportion faced unemployment.[13] The number of employment opportunities requiring university training had not kept pace with the number of university graduates. Moreover, the French have historically enrolled in the humanities and social sciences in disproportionately high numbers, and France in the 1960s had few jobs for humanists and social scientists. French students had every reason to view the employment situation with alarm.

The archaic character of the French educational system played directly into the hands of the critics. The inflexible centralization of the French university is difficult to fathom. All decisions about financial allocations, faculty resources, and curriculums are made in the ministry of education in Paris and promulgated on a nationwide basis. The result is "a hierarchy of disciplines dating from Auguste Comte and of faculty structures inherited from the Empire."[14] This obsolete uniformity was compounded by a pervasive sense of impotence on the part of students, faculty, and administrators. There was no room for negotiation, reform, or compromise.

Further exacerbating the situation was the insensitivity and authoritarianism of the administrators and faculty members. Attached to the rules of seniority and privilege, these groups were singularly arrogant and remote. Writes Aron: "Every professor was supreme master of his chair below God. An unreasonable professor could paralyze the system; no one could oblige anyone to do anything, the Minister of National Education . . . had no intellectual or pedagogic authority at all. . . . Not even the dean of the university could force a recalcitrant professor to adopt a reasonable organization of studies in his department."[15]

There arose in this atmosphere an articulate core of intellectuals and student leaders to attack the educational system and demand meaningful reform. Powerful sentiments set loose by the war in Vietnam fed the discontent and mobilized the students by the thousands.

The disgruntled segments of French society saw the government of Charles de Gaulle as the cause of their frustration and discontent. The values held by large numbers of students and workers were diametrically opposed to the values of the General. The students wanted a new university system with a modern curriculum; de Gaulle wanted to expand France's nuclear power. The workers wanted more control over working conditions; de Gaulle was interested only in increased productivity as a means of improving France's economic position in the world market. The widening cleavage between de Gaulle and segments of French society was quite pronounced. The paternalistic, olympian style of the General's rule infuriated the youth of the country and betrayed a government out of tune with the times.

The fossilized, stifling bureaucracy of the Fifth Republic —a relic of Napoleonic times—persistently called attention to the disjunction between old structures and new needs. France became a "stalled society." As such, the "spirit of May" was a challenge not simply to Charles de Gaulle, but to the fabric of the French sociopolitical system.

The conditions that predisposed France to political revolution in 1968 are not qualitatively different from those in other prerevolutionary societies. The uniqueness of the French Revolution of 1968 stems from the fact that for the first time a large-scale revolutionary struggle broke out in a modern industrial society. To this topic we shall return in Chapter 7.

LEADERSHIP

In a sharp departure from traditional thinking, the French revolutionaries denied the existence of and the need for leadership in revolution. Indeed, contemptuous of leadership (and, as we shall see, organization), they glorified "spontaneity."

The most articulate spokesman for this point of view is undoubtedly Daniel Cohn-Bendit, who expresses the conviction that "the revolutionary cannot and must not be a leader." A most remarkable phenomenon about the events of May, he argues, "was the spontaneity of the resistance —a clear sign that our movement does not need leaders to direct it; that it can perfectly well express itself without the help of a 'vanguard.'" Cohn-Bendit vigorously attacks Lenin's conception of a vanguard party on the grounds that, being imposed from above and outside, it stifles self-involvement, direct action, and spontaneity. Leadership, he firmly believes, becomes bureaucratized, self-perpetuating, corrupt, unresponsive, and separated from the masses.[16]

The May revolution was the work not of a vanguard party but of an "active minority" that detonated the movement without attempting to direct and control it. The strength of the movement lies in an "uncontrollable spontaneity." Cohn-Bendit said in his famous interview with Jean-Paul Sartre in late May 1968:

> What has happened in the last fortnight is to my mind a refutation of the famous theory of the "revolutionary vanguard" as the force leading a popular movement. . . . The active minority was able to light the fuse and make the breach. . . . But from then on no vanguard[s] . . . have been able to seize control of the movement. . . . They have been drowned in the movement. . . .
>
> This is the essential point. It shows that we must abandon the theory of the "leading vanguard" and replace it by a much simpler and more honest one of the active minority functioning as a permanent leaven, pushing for action without ever leading it. . . . Spontaneity makes possible the forward drive, not the orders of a leading group. . . .
>
> Our movement's strength is precisely that it is based on an "uncontrollable spontaneity," that it gives an impetus without trying to canalize it or to use the action it has unleashed to its own profit.[17]

Other leaders of the May revolution qualify Cohn-Bendit's view. For example, Alain Geismar says of Cohn-Bendit's March 22 Movement that "It has a number of 'leaders' in the sociological sense of the term, but no 'officials,' no executives, even less bureaucracy."[18] Jacques Sauvageot stresses the collective nature of leadership. In response to the questions, "Do you really work as a team?

Aren't you afraid that you have lapsed into a personality cult?" he stated, "The press needs an official spokesman, a 'gimmick,' but in reality we do work as a team, and anyway we are trying more and more to express ourselves in collective statements." He thought, in contrast to Cohn-Bendit, that spontaneity and direction "are not incompatible. It is possible both to let the base [i.e., mass] express itself and to attempt to structure the movement." Stressing the dangers of centralization he added, "I believe in mass spontaneity, but also in the necessity of organizations able to make the mass aware."[19]

The leaders of the May revolution, then, disagree on the nature of revolutionary leadership and its relation to spontaneity. However, the May revolution was neither completely spontaneous nor planned and engineered in the same sense and to the same degree as the revolutions in Bolivia and Vietnam. Leadership and planning did play a part. Hervé Bourges is correct when he writes, "Officially the movement has no leadership. . . . But still, a dozen militants with no special prerogatives do stand out, no doubt because of their energy, their tactical sense, and their understanding of situations."[20]

The most outstanding leaders of the May revolution were Alain Geismar, Jacques Sauvageot, Alain Krivine, and Daniel Cohn-Bendit—all members of the so-called revolutionary high command (see below), a loosely knit group characterized by considerable internal disagreement. Among the lesser leaders (not discussed in this chapter due to lack of data) are Jean-Pierre Duteuil, 22, a sociology student at Nanterre and a member of the March 22 Movement; Marc Kravetz and Jean-Louis Peninou, both 26, of the Mouvement d'Action Universitaire; Michel Recanati, 17, of Comité d'Action Lycéen; and the physicist Jean-Pierre Vigier, 40, of the Comité Vietnam National.

The former general secretary of the National Union of Higher Education (Syndicat National de l'Enseignement Supérieur), Alain Geismar was born in 1939 to middle-class parents. He is a tranquil, self-confident Marxist who "betrays nothing suggesting revolutionary torment."[21] A professor of physics at the Faculty of Science in Paris,

Geismar attracted prestigious academics to support the student movement. He did not hesitate to involve his union in revolutionary struggle; and, when his union office became something of a constraint, he resigned his post in order to devote full attention to political action. Geismar was impatient with bureaucracy and highly critical of the French Communist Party. He called for a radical transformation of the university. He publicized and exploited every clumsy move on the part of the authorities.

Another member of the high command is Jacques Sauvageot. Born in Dijon of middle-class background, 25 at the time of the revolution, Sauvageot was vice-president of the National Union of French Students (Union Nationale des Étudiants de France). A student of art history, he was engaged at the time of the revolution in a research project on a nineteenth-century painter. Sauvageot played a particularly important role in co-ordinating student efforts and limiting the scope of the confrontation with the police.

Alain Krivine was born in 1941, the son of a well-to-do Jewish dentist. A brilliant history student at the Sorbonne, he is "very calm and self-possessed. His most striking qualities are relentless clarity, great fluency, and the sort of realism rarely found in extremist politics."[22] Krivine became active in Communist youth groups early in life and played a leading role in the formation of the Revolutionary Communist Youth (Jeunesse Communiste Révolutionnaire).

Daniel Cohn-Bendit is the most outstanding leader/ideologue of the French Revolution of 1968. He was at the time of the revolution 23 years old and a second-year sociology student at Nanterre. Cohn-Bendit was born in France, his father a German refugee. Following a secondary education in Paris, he returned to Germany to attend school, where he chose German citizenship. Having enrolled at Nanterre, he was granted a renewable visa, the revocation of which was considered on several occasions during the months of May and June 1968. He, too, is said to have been a brilliant student.

Cohn-Bendit is a Marxist-anarchist, equally contemptuous

of bourgeois society and the French Communist Party. He symbolically united the two flags so prominently displayed throughout the May revolution: the red flag of socialism and the black flag of anarchism. Cohn-Bendit functioned as an important transmitter to French students of the ideas and techniques of the German SDS (Sozialistischer Deutscher Studentenbund). A person of considerable charisma, he was particularly good at mobilizing the uncommitted, and particularly adept at rhetoric.

In summary the leaders of the French Revolution of 1968 were surprisingly young, most of them in their twenties. They came from the middle and upper-middle social strata. They were very well educated, most of them being university students or professors. The main characteristics of the French leaders are reported in Table 6.1.

IDEOLOGY

The French Revolution of 1968 was dominated by a number of groups, organizations, and leaders, many of whom espoused more or less distinct (though fragmentary) ideologies. Even Daniel Cohn-Bendit, who denied the importance of ideology and warned of its paralyzing effects,[23] proposed an explicit ideology of revolutionary insurrection. Although there was little ideological uniformity in France in 1968, it is possible to construct a composite profile of the ideology of the May revolution. Such a profile can be misleading, since it imputes to the French revolutionary ideology a coherence and unity that it in fact lacks. Approached with caution, however, the ideological profile sketched below will contribute toward an understanding of the French Revolution of 1968.

The ideology of the May revolution has three principal components: a critique of the existing order, a vision of an alternative order, and a statement of means or instruments necessary to implement the alternative order. Before considering each in turn, it is necessary to clarify the influence of Herbert Marcuse on the ideology of the May

TABLE 6.1

PROFILE OF FRENCH LEADERS

Characteristic	Cohn-Bendit	Geismar	Sauvageot	Krivine
Date of birth	1945	1939	1943	1941
Age in 1968	23	29	25	27
Place of birth	S.E. France	?	Dijon	?
Social origin	Middle class?	Middle class	Middle class	Middle class
Occupation	Student leader	Professor	Student leader	Student leader
		Secy.-Gen./SNESup	Vice-Pres./UNEF	
Education	University	University	University	University
Foreign exposure	Extensive	Moderate	Moderate	Moderate

revolution, for the subject has generated much controversy. Put directly, Marcuse appears to have been of little or no consequence. A French edition of *One Dimensional Man* (1964) was published in France only in mid-May 1968, when the struggle was already well underway. Some of the key leaders of the revolution denied having read Marcuse. Alain Geismar said in an interview that, although many have regarded Marcuse as the harbinger of a new social order, "I must say that, to my knowledge, none of the militants in my union . . . or in any other organization, with the possible exception of one in a thousand, has ever read a line of this author who is presented to us as the great precursor to the struggle taking place in universities the world over."[24] Cohn-Bendit stated flatly, "Some people have tried to force Marcuse on us as a mentor: that is a joke. None of us have read Marcuse. . . . No writer could be regarded as the inspiration of the movement."[25]

The French revolutionaries had of course read Marx, Bakunin, Lenin, Trotsky, Mao, Guevara, and Sartre, as well as the contemporary French Marxist philosopher Henri Lefebvre, a professor at Nanterre. And, through Cohn-Bendit, they had been exposed to the ideas and techniques of the German SDS. The most that can be said, however, is that there is a certain affinity or correspondence among Marxist critiques of industrial society—be they advanced by Lefebvre, Marcuse, or the SDS—but Marcuse alone did not provide the primary ideological impetus of the May revolution.

The critique of the existing order begins with a frontal assault upon the university and proceeds to a critique of society at large. The student revolutionaries attacked the university for treating education as "a marketable commodity" and subordinating intellectual integrity to the needs of an exploitative economic system. Announcing their determination "to reject any ideological subjection," they took sharp issue with Christian Fouchet, the former minister of education, who had called for the "industrialization" of the university in order to meet the educational and training needs of business, the professions, and industry.[26] Daniel Cohn-Bendit put the matter succinctly:

> . . . [T]he basis of university education [is] the preparation of a privileged minority for a return to the ranks of the ruling class from which they have taken temporary leave of absence. The university has, in fact, become a sausage-machine which turns out people without any real culture, and incapable of thinking for themselves, but trained to fit into the economic system of a highly industrialized society. The student . . . is being fed "culture" as a goose is fed grain—to be sacrificed on the altar of bourgeois appetites.[27]

The students, then, see the university as an appendage of the modern industrial state, and education as an instrument in the service of the economy and the polity. Education creates and molds the specialized personnel required by modern production; it integrates these personnel into the fabric of bourgeois exploitation and indoctrinates them with the ideology of the status quo. According to Jacques Sauvageot, "today the university trains cadres who participate in one way or another in the maintenance of the capitalist system, especially by becoming society's watchdogs, spreading the ideology of the ruling class."[28] Equally blunt in his criticism, Cohn-Bendit specifically attacks "sociology as a capitalist fraud" for its celebration of the status quo. He condemns sociology, political sociology, and social psychology for their persistent attempts to mold and condition man to accept existing society, for their preoccupation with fitting man to machine rather than vice versa.[29]

Capitalism, the revolutionaries believe, has entered a monopolistic, bureaucratic stage. Neocapitalist society attempts to hide its exploitative nature under the guise of "rationality." This rationality, however, is a rationality of profit, not of human needs. Though thoroughly oppressive, bureaucratic capitalism is capable of co-opting some of its critics by spreading a portion of the material wealth. "The fact is that for fifteen years the bourgeoisie has been buying off the lower classes by offering or promising more consumer goods, education, social promotion. . . . TV, household appliances, cars become urgent needs and symbols of promotion."[30] In a subtle play on an old Marxist dictum, a Sorbonne wall slogan captured the thrust of this criticism: "Commodities are the opium of the people." In a word, bureaucratic capitalism hides its exploitative, intolerant nature behind a façade of liberalism and reasonableness. It is in fact a closed society, incapable of "qualitative change." The only way to deal with it is to smash it by force. Writes Cohn-Bendit:

> . . . [W]e are not so much protesting that our education is out of touch with the needs of the future, nor complaining about the shortage of jobs; we totally reject the entire system. Our protest only turns into violent action because the structure of society cannot be smashed by talk or ballot papers. . . .
>
> As a result, the student movement has become revolutionary and not simply a university protest. It does not rule out reforms (its actions, in fact, provoke them) but it tries beyond its immediate aims to elaborate a strategy that will radically change the whole of society.[31]

Neocapitalist exploitation extends beyond its national boundaries to embrace the Third World. Anti-imperialism has been a characteristic, of course, of the student movement world wide. Veterans of the protest movement against the Algerian War and well read in Marxist literature, the French revolutionaries considered American involvement in Vietnam as a decisive confrontation between imperialism and the colonial revolutions. To them, the Vietnam War symbolized a sick Western society of which France is an integral part. Vietnam served to cement thousands of young people in schools and universities, because it seemed to dramatize the violence of neocapitalism. Representing the fulfillment of the prophecies of Marx, Mao, and others, Vietnam far surpassed the Algerian War as a mobilizer of radical sentiments. The ideology of the May revolution, in short, was shaped by events not entirely indigenous to France.

One of the striking features of the ideology of May is a profound disdain for traditional politics—whether rightist, leftist, or centrist. In the revolutionaries' view, no political party—liberal, conservative, socialist, or Communist—is capable of presenting a point of view sufficiently progressive to remedy the shortcomings of neocapitalist society. All political parties are necessarily corrupt, bureaucratized, hierarchical, and unresponsive. Contemptuous of politics and politicians, the French revolutionaries delighted in excluding leading political personalities from their rallies and demonstrations, or else giving them a back seat. Said Cohn-Bendit, "To bring real politics [i.e., mass action] into everyday life is to get rid of the [traditional] politicians."[32]

Parliamentarianism is to no avail; it is a "gimmick" and an ally of bureaucratic capitalism. Writes Jean-Pierre Vigier, "What is now clear to all who are serious about revolutionary change is that the parliamentary game is futile. For several generations the French bourgeoisie has used elections and the plebiscite to legitimize their power. But these institutions were meant to civilize the demands of non-integrated groups and make them more palatable. Parliaments recast demands in forms acceptable to existing society."[33] Elections, according to Cohn-Bendit, constitute "a magic ritual. . . . My personal viewpoint is that revolutionary struggle should take almost no notice of votes. Direct action in factory and street is what will change the situation, not electoral majorities."[34] The revolutionary struggle, in other words, is totally at variance with bourgeois democracy.

The French revolutionaries were as unsparing in their criticism of the parties of the left, and especially of the Parti Communiste Français (PCF), as they were of other political parties.[35] The PCF, the revolutionaries charged, had become a party of the established order, a defender of the status quo, and completely subservient to the Moscow line. Reformist and counterrevolutionary, it had evolved into an authoritarian, regimented, obsolescent establishment no longer responsive to the needs and demands of those who supported it.

The traditional parties of the left, the revolutionaries

charged, had come to accept the neocapitalist society and seek integration within bourgeois parliamentarianism. They had become, in the words of Geismar, "capitalism's loyal managers: ready to organize it, but opposed to qualitative leaps."[36] The PCF leaders had come to believe that change could be accomplished at the ballot box. They wished to come to power, to be sure, but in a strictly legal and legitimate way. Failing to understand the May revolution, they denounced the student militants as "anarchist," "adventurist," "Trotskyite," "Maoist," "Castroite," "Guevarist," and "pseudo-revolutionary." They supported the moderate students who sought reconciliation with the university authorities and the Gaullist regime. In short, Geismar charged, the PCF had emerged as the "anti-communist structure par excellence."[37]

The French revolutionaries, then, sought to smash the existing order in the interest of a better society; they sought to do away with neocapitalism, bureaucratic corruption, and depersonalized authority. But what were their positive goals and objectives? What was their image of the alternative society?

Some of the revolutionary leaders denied that a positive program was necessary, and others refused to specify goals. Stanley Hoffman quotes a young activist to have said, "The revolutionaries are men without a program."[38] When asked about his conception of the ideal society, Alain Geismar simply stated, "The movement will find itself en route."[39] For this group of revolutionaries, as Hoffman suggests, action and movement were ends in themselves.

A more articulate group of revolutionary leaders did attempt to spell out programs and objectives. "What we must agree on," writes Cohn-Bendit, "are the general principles of the society we want to create."[40] The leaders of the May revolution were held together by a number of ideals, of which the most important were self-management and direct democracy. The revolutionaries sought a decentralized, debureaucratized, egalitarian, "classless" society in which men control their own fate. They wished to humanize society by putting an end to oppression and ex-

ploitation and by giving full play to self-expression, freedom, and spontaneity. They preached self-management
by students in the universities, by workers in the factories.

Cohn-Bendit believes that the technological advances of
neocapitalism should be employed "to gain greater mastery
over the environment." Bureaucratic capitalism should be
replaced by a more human system stressing social justice
and political liberty. Direct democracy should become the
order of the day: in the polity, self-government by all; in
the economy, self-management by the workers; in the university, self-rule by the students. What would the principal
structures of the ideal society be like? "I think a federation
of workers' councils, soviets, a classless society, a society
where the social division of labor between manual and intellectual workers no longer exists. As to the precise forms
of organization, they cannot be defined yet. But there are
examples, historical models."[41]

Such far-reaching changes, Cohn-Bendit maintains, cannot be attained without a change in man. That, in fact, is
an ultimate objective: "The real meaning of the revolution is not a change in management, but a change in man.
This change we must make in our own lifetime and not for
our children's sake, for the revolution must be born of joy
and not of sacrifice."[42]

The last sentence brings to light another striking characteristic of the May revolution: the extraordinary romanticism that pervaded it and at times threatened to drown
it. Some of this romanticism is captured in the slogans that
adorned the walls of the Sorbonne and the Latin Quarter:
"Create." "Power to the imagination." "Be a realist, demand the impossible." "It is forbidden to forbid."[43]

Some writers have used such terms as joy, exhilaration,
and delirium to describe the state of mind of the revolutionaries. Stanley Hoffman writes that the revolution was in
part "a moving orgy of face-to-face relations, a sudden,
joyous, noisy release from silence and isolation, a delirium
of stream-of-consciousness discussions, debates, dia-
logues."[44] Two eyewitnesses give the following account of
the Night of the Barricades:

Boys and girls threw themselves into the fighting with incredible abandon and dedication. To many young and high-keyed spirits, this was the chance to join the heroic revolution of Frantz Fanon, Che Guevara, Régis Debray, to which they had so long thrilled. This was their Vietnam. . . . In deadly earnest, they were playing a game of guerrillas, acting out the colonial revolution in the heart of a Western capital.[45]

Another writer agrees: "For the young, Che Guevara and the Vietnamese guerrilla were now in their midst. Guerrilla combat took place in front of the very neon signs that beckoned youth to invest its energy in the palliatives built by adult society."[46] Cohn-Bendit crystallizes the symbolism of the Night of the Barricades in the following fashion:

The barricades were no longer simply a means of self-defense, they became a symbol of individual liberty. This is why the night of 10 May can never be forgotten by those who were "there." For bourgeois historians the barricades will doubtless become symbols of senseless violence, but for the students themselves they represented a turning point that should have its place among the great moments of history. The memory of the raids, the gas grenades, the wounds and the injuries will surely remain, but we will also remember that night for the exemplary bravery of the "communards" or "sans culottes" of the rue Gay-Lussac, of young men and women who opened a new and cleaner page in the history of France.[47]

Although necessarily exaggerated, the romanticism of the May revolution performed the primary function of restoring to the participants a feeling of unity and spontaneity. It symbolized an open rebellion against neocapitalism and the creation of a community in the midst of a corrupt bourgeois society.

The reference to spontaneity highlights another strand of revolutionary ideology: anarchism. This is well illustrated in the prevalence with which the black flag was flown side by side with the red flag throughout the May revolution. Anarchism is a particular characteristic of Cohn-Bendit, whose distaste for leadership we have already examined and whose disdain for organization will soon become apparent. Cohn-Bendit sought simply to trigger events with no intention to control or direct them. "The movement's only chance," he said, "is the disorder that lets men speak freely."[48] Part of the reason for Cohn-Bendit's idealization of "uncontrollable spontaneity" may lie in the sheer inability of the revolutionaries to control the movement they had initiated.

Less complimentary interpretations of the romanticism of the May revolution have been put forward by some authors, most notably Raymond Aron. Basically, Aron argues, the May revolution was a "psychodrama" in which the students acted out their loneliness, frustrations, illusions, deprivations, and shortcomings. Describing the revolution variously as "collective madness" and a "vast charade," Aron writes, "Paris . . . rehearsed once again the Great Revolution. I use the word 'rehearse' in its theatrical sense. . . . The actors re-ran the play, merely acting, whereas the real actors of 1789 . . . changed the course of history. Once again the French people, obsessed by their memories or the myths of their past, mistook riot and disorder in the streets for a Promethean exploit." The embittered Aron comes down very hard on the student revolutionaries: "To dislocate the social bloc of the university without knowing what kind of new social structure to build, or with the intention of dislocating the whole society, is nothing but aesthetic nihilism, or, rather, an outburst by barbarians who are unaware of their barbarity."[49]

Such, at any rate, were the goals of the French revolutionaries. What means did they propose toward the realization of these goals?

A principal key to an understanding of the ideology of May is the concept of *contestation*.[50] Without a precise English equivalent, the term denotes the combined meanings of contest, provocation, challenge, and struggle. Rejecting the bourgeois slogans of parliamentarianism, accommodation, adjustment, and compromise, *contestation* aims at the revolutionary seizure of power throughout society.

The French revolutionaries undertook *contestation permanente:* unceasing agitation and harassment to undermine the existing social order and unite the forces of revolution. They practiced *contestation globale:* the struggle begun in the universities was to engulf society at large and the international community as well. In a word, the revolutionaries saw the student struggle as a permanent struggle on a world-wide scale.

Contestation necessarily rests on action—another idealized term in the vocabulary of the May revolution. Action takes various forms: strikes, demonstrations, occupations. But action is not the same as violence: "Violence is one means of action, but we don't have a cult of violence. However, there are moments when the relation of [social] forces is such that violence becomes a necessity."[51]

In order to give reality to the principle of action, "action committees" were created in the universities, factories, neighborhoods, shops, and communities throughout France. They were viewed as means of realigning the social forces, as revolutionary substitutes for political parties and trade unions. They were seen as open challenges to capitalist society, as foundations of "dual power" separating revolution and reaction. They were "the embryo organizations of the new society."[52]

Contestation, the revolutionaries believed, serves to mobilize the great masses of the uncommitted. It radicalizes the students to challenge the educational system, reject the routine of lectures and examinations, occupy the universities, and provoke the authorities to undertake repressive action. It radicalizes the workers to strike, take over the running of the factories, and provoke the management and union officials. Repressive action by university and state authorities further mobilizes the population and generates sympathy for the revolutionaries. Meanwhile, without its universities and factories neocapitalist society cannot survive. "Although it would strictly be possible for troops to take over a number of social functions, the . . . [police] cannot substitute itself for skilled workers to make the factories go, students to pass examinations, or teachers to teach courses."[53]

The student revolutionaries, it is clear, did not entertain the idea of making a revolution on their own. A chief function of *contestation* was to mobilize and politicize the masses to help make the revolution. In particular, the revolutionaries sought unity with the working class. Cohn-Bendit called for the abolition of the distinction between workers and intellectuals.[54] Jacques Sauvageot demanded that student power and workers' power be established simultaneously: "The formula 'student power' . . . must be defined in relation to 'workers' power': the factory to the workers, the university to the students."[55]

The revolutionaries spared no effort to reach the workers directly and to convince them of the identity of their interests with those of the students. Since the mid-1960s they had sought employment in factories and lower-class vacation camps. They had capitalized on the authoritarianism of the Gaullist regime, the unresponsiveness of social and political institutions, and the uncertainties of the economy. They had organized "long marches" to the factories, most particularly to Boulogne-Billancourt, the main Renault factory, on the outskirts of Paris, employing some thirty thousand workers. In fact, the Boulogne-Billancourt emerged as the symbolic counterpart of the Sorbonne.

In these activities the students were not disappointed. Buoyed by the full involvement of the workers in the May revolution, Cohn-Bendit stated, "The working class has proved its combativity. . . . The revolutionary nucleus has grown and tomorrow it will constitute a firm point of departure."[56]

To summarize, the ideology of the May revolution is rooted in a rejection of the existing order and the projection of an alternative society. The vision of the alternative society combines the teachings of classical democracy, socialism, anarchism, and romanticism. The means are *contestation*, action, provocation, student/worker unity. It is one of the peculiarities of the May revolution that it united those who wanted more of the consumer society with those who rejected it.

ORGANIZATION

Although the French revolutionaries openly challenged the need for organization, much of this challenge is superficial and collapses under scrutiny. Daniel Cohn-Bendit, for example, presents a contradictory point of view. On the one hand, he warns, "we must avoid building an organization immediately, or defining a program; that would inevitably paralyze us. The movement's only chance is the disorder that lets men speak freely, and which can result in a form of self-organization." On the other, he calls for the creation of "revolutionary organisms," "action committees," and a "host of insurrectional cells" to make possible self-expression at the grass roots and to carry the struggle to colleges and universities, shops and factories. "All revolutionary activity is collective," he writes, "and hence involves a degree of organization. What we challenge is not the need for this but the need for a revolutionary leadership, the need for a party."[57] It appears, then, that Cohn-Bendit is not against organization as such, but against old-style organizations that, imposed from above, stifle spontaneity. "Organization is not an end in itself, but an evolving means of coping with specific situations."[58] It must be continually remolded and reshaped to fit the needs of the times.

The French Revolution of 1968 was not fully "spontaneous" by any stretch of the imagination, though it was more spontaneous than most. A plethora of organizations representing nearly every shade of opinion along the Marxist-leftist-militant continuum played dominant roles in the struggle. Of these organizations, the most important are the March 22 Movement (Mouvement du 22 Mars), the National Union of Higher Education (Syndicat National de l'Enseignement Supérieur, SNESup), the National Union of French Students (Union Nationale des

Étudiants de France, UNEF), the University Action Movement (Mouvement d'Action Universitaire, MAU), the Revolutionary Communist Youth (Jeunesse Communiste Révolutionnaire, JCR), and the Union of French Communist Youth—Marxist-Leninist (Union de la Jeunesse Communiste—Marxiste-Léniniste, UJC-ML).

The principal organization responsible for initiating agitation, sparking the revolution, and maintaining its momentum was the March 22 Movement. Organized by Cohn-Bendit at Nanterre on March 22, 1968, the Movement was a response to a series of student protests, dating back to the fall of 1967, against the outdated system of French education and its alleged complicity with neocapitalism. The Movement, powerfully fed by anti-Vietnam War sentiment, began with a core of 142 students and quickly spread to large segments of the Nanterre student body, particularly after the introduction of police on campus early in 1968.

Considering itself "a political movement, not a student movement," and stressing its unity with the working class, March 22 sought a total restructuring of the university, leading to a transformation of society at large. Making "no distinction between leaders and led," the Movement's "very structure was opposed to the Bolshevik conception of a proletarian vanguard."[59] Consisting of leftists of all sorts—Marxist, Trotskyite, Maoist, Guevarist, anarchist— the March 22 Movement was in a sense a microcosm of Cohn-Bendit's vision of the good society: free, spontaneous, egalitarian.

The National Union of Higher Education (SNESup) is an organization of junior faculty members representing about one third of the university professors. Its members feel a sense of affinity with the students not only because of the proximity in age but also because their role in the French university system is neither very prestigious nor very powerful; indeed, they do not even enjoy sufficient autonomy to teach the courses they wish. Under Alain Geismar's direction, the SNESup played a vital role in mobilizing the French intellectuals. Its offices became the headquarters and communications center for the May revolution.

As a mobilizer of French youth, the National Union of French Students (UNEF) was no newcomer to the political scene. According to vice-president Jacques Sauvageot, the UNEF is a student union to the extent that it is "charged with the defense of students and their professional training. . . . But I believe that given the realities of the student situation the UNEF is primarily a movement of progressive youth."[60] Founded after World War II, and led by left-wing Catholics, the UNEF played a decisive part in organizing student protest against the Algerian War. This activity cost the organization its "official" standing and government subsidy. It also created dissension within UNEF and encouraged the government to sponsor a rival student union. Membership shrank badly.

The Vietnam War and the May revolution breathed new life into the UNEF. In the late 1960s the organization claimed a membership of over seventy thousand and believed that about one half of French university students looked to it for leadership. During the May crisis, UNEF completely lost its identity as a student union and became a full-fledged political force. Student politics, its leaders argued, are inseparable from politics in general. According to Sauvageot, UNEF's principal role during the May revolution was that of a spokesman, or "megaphone, defining a number of aims, advancing a number of propositions. . . . It also acted as a coordinating center. The fact that the movement grew in the provinces was due to UNEF action."[61]

In March 1968, a militant wing of the Fédération des Groupes d'Études de Lettres—itself a UNEF section in the Sorbonne faculty of letters—broke off and formed the Mouvement d'Action Universitaire. MAU leaders consisted for the most part of experienced and politically mature graduate students and research workers. They constituted "a Sorbonne Marxist elite, unaffiliated with any party, high-minded, humane."[62] MAU leaders immediately identified with the March 22 Movement because they shared some of Cohn-Bendit's views. They played a key role in mobilizing college and university students.

The Revolutionary Communist Youth (JCR) and the Union of French Communist Youth—Marxist-Leninist (UJC-ML) are composed of militants formerly affiliated with the Union des Étudiants Communistes (UEC). Established in the mid-1950s, the UEC is the youth group of the Communist Party. The founders of the JCR and the UJC-ML had been purged from the UEC in 1965 following a long series of clashes with the PCF leadership over the latter's anti-revolutionary stance.

Founded in April 1966, the JCR is a tightly knit, well-disciplined organization patterned after the teachings of Trotsky and Lenin. JCR leaders gave first priority to the formation of a vanguard revolutionary party, for they firmly believed that without such a party no revolution could materialize. Within two years, they had turned the JCR into a formidable political force.

As can be seen, in many respects the JCR stands in sharp contrast to the March 22 Movement, with which it formed an alliance early in the struggle. In fact, the JCR gave the March 22 "unconditional support" because it recognized the potentially explosive nature of Cohn-Bendit's teachings, which the JCR intended to exploit to its own ends. The two organizations had in common a belief in the violent overthrow of the Gaullist regime.

The mass of the French working class, the JCR recognized, had remained faithful to the Communist Party. The only way to wean the workers was from inside the PCF and in particular from inside its dependent trade union, the Confédération Générale du Travail (CGT). Many members of the JCR went to work in the factories in order to gain access to workers and spread the revolution. When the crisis exploded in May, the JCR played an important part in street demonstrations and at the barricades.

The UJC-ML was founded in November 1966 by the expelled Maoist militants of the UEC. Austere and spartan, the UJC-ML leaders adopted the slogan of *Servir le Peuple*,[63] particularly the workers and the students. They quickly insinuated themselves into the factories in order to reach the workers with the teachings of Mao. They devoted considerable attention to organizing and mobilizing lycée and university students and linking them with the workers.

The UJC-ML initially distrusted the March 22 Movement and denounced it as reactionary. In April 1968, however, the UJC-ML did a complete turnabout and publicly confessed its error: "We had preconceived sectarian ideas about student movements because they so rarely succeed. But we have now decided to merge with the March 22 like fish in water."[64] (Note another Maoist allusion.)

In addition to the organizations just described, a host of groups and committees were quite prominent in the French Revolution of 1968. In 1966–67, the leftist militants had created the Comité Vietnam National and the Comité Vietnam de Base to help mobilize a larger public, particularly in the colleges and universities. These groups were soon joined by a network of school-based Comités d'Action Lycéens (CALs), specifically set up to reach the teen-age population. Operating under the slogan of "Freedom of expression in school," the CALs agitated, boycotted classes, disrupted examinations, participated in strikes, and harassed the police. Thousands of lycée students proved every bit as militant as their university counterparts.

Following the Night of the Barricades, thousands of grass-roots action committees sprang up throughout France (some 450 in Paris alone) as a means of giving expression to "direct democracy" and "direct action." "Never before," wrote Cohn-Bendit, "had the local population been so actively involved in real political decisions; never before were their voices heard so clearly in the public forum. Democracy sprang from discussion of our immediate needs and the exigencies of the situation which demanded action." The functions of the action committees, according to Cohn-Bendit, were to share in the fighting, reinforce the strikers' pickets, distribute food, print and distribute leaflets and posters, facilitate communication, organize meetings, unite the workers and students, mobilize the uncommitted, and generate a sense of community. They showed, Cohn-Bendit asserted, that leadership, organization, political parties, and trade unions were completely unnecessary.[65] Jean-Pierre Vigier maintained that they were the prototype of a new society and "the most important political innovation of the May Revolution."[66]

The organizations described in the foregoing pages confronted a series of difficulties throughout the May revolution. For one thing, the spate of organizations (many lesser ones have not even been mentioned here) without a central co-ordinating unit hampered effective leadership and action. For another, although united in their opposition to the government of Charles de Gaulle, these organizations were ridden by factionalism, division, and interorganizational rivalry. For example, the UJC-ML distrusted virtually all the other organizations. The March 22 Movement attacked UNEF for operating within a bourgeois framework. The authorities made every effort to manipulate the revolutionary organizations against one another. They played the more "responsible" ones (for example, UNEF) against the more militant ones (the March 22, the UJC-ML).

In their attempt to politicize, mobilize, and unite with the workers, the students faced a formidable task in the solid opposition of the trade unions and the parties of the left, particularly the CGT and the PCF. Representing 50 per cent of the organized French workers, the CGT is under complete Communist control. (The CGT secretary-general is a member of the PCF central committee.) The CGT and the PCF had become reformist, fully integrated into the French bourgeois society. They sought a bigger share of the economic pie, not the destruction of the capitalist system. They sought political power, but only at the polls. The French trade unions, Cohn-Bendit believed, had become a part of the "loyal opposition"; the PCF had betrayed its revolutionary past and turned counterrevolutionary.[67] André Barjonet—a high-ranking CGT official who resigned on May 23, 1968, as "a gesture of protest against the organization's failure in its revolutionary vocation"—attacked the CGT and the PCF for their inability to understand the May revolution ("because it was not in the program"), their hostile attitude toward the students, and their "resolute parliamentarianism."[68]

The CGT and the PCF vigorously opposed the May revolution and made every effort to subvert it.[69] They resisted every attempt by the student leaders to draw the workers into the struggle. They opposed the idea of a general strike because it might disrupt the economy, alienate the voters, and damage their chances in the next elections. They went along with the twenty-four-hour general strike only after they had become convinced, in part by the restlessness and militancy of the younger workers, that it was bound to take place. Cohn-Bendit is probably justified when he writes that the PCF and the CGT "were forced, willy nilly, to call a general strike for 13 May 1968, in an attempt to take the political sting out of the student movement."[70] Even then, the PCF and the CGT used the strike simply to press economic demands. Thus when trade-union leaders met with Premier Pompidou on May 25–27, they anxiously accepted the government's concessions, only to be turned down by the workers. They continued to urge the workers to return to work.

Anticipating the fall of the de Gaulle government and the possibility of new elections, the PCF in late May called for a "popular government." Seizing the initiative on May 30, President de Gaulle successfully raised the specter of "totalitarian communism" to mobilize the French people and subsequently score an overwhelming victory at the polls.

TERROR AND VIOLENCE

The use of terror and violence as a conscious means of facilitating and implementing revolutionary objectives was virtually non-existent in the May revolution. In the early weeks of the struggle, physical damage and destruction in both the Sorbonne and the Latin Quarter were minimal.

In the later weeks, groups of students surged forth from their sanctuaries in the Sorbonne to smash windows and set fire to cars (and in one case to a police station nearby), but these "spontaneous" and isolated acts did not typify the movement, which by that time had already spent itself.

Several considerations account for the absence of revolutionary terror in the May revolution. Events unfolded in an extremely rapid and unexpected fashion; few revolutionaries (or anyone else, for that matter) had anticipated the dimensions of the conflict they ignited. The revolutionaries lacked a co-ordinating mechanism to plan and implement revolutionary terror. They lacked the physical means of mounting effective violence: few had firearms, and even fewer seem to have used them. Paving stones and street signs, though plentiful, were simply no match for the implements available to the authorities.

On the other hand, governmental terror and violence were quite prominent throughout the May revolution. Some of this violence was provoked by the students themselves, who were intent upon a policy of mobilizing the uncommitted by exposing the repressive nature of the Gaullist regime. In this, they were not disappointed by the authorities.

By every available account, the French police employed indiscriminate force, not only against the students and factory workers but against the general population as well. Police brutality, writes Cohn-Bendit, is "well documented: houses were broken into; young people rounded up at gunpoint; and afterwards in the cells, there were beatings and sadistic tortures."[71] An expert on the French police wrote of the "policemen who tear into demonstrators, beat up young people under arrest in police stations, burst into cafes, restaurants or private houses, and dedicate themselves to a brutal manhunt."[72] Eyewitnesses told of indiscriminate police beatings and clubbings, breaking into private premises, and even collective rape; the whole thing, said an older woman, reminded her of the Nazi occupation.[73] The Washington *Post* commented in retrospect that "The behavior of [French] policemen who delight in beating up not only demonstrators, but innocent passers-by, has become a major scandal."[74]

Much of the governmental violence was launched by a specially trained unit, Companies Républicaines de Sécurité (CRS). The large-scale brutality to which the CRS resorted helped unite the students and bring forth the wrath of the French people. Scrawled all over the Latin Quarter was one of the bitterest of the student slogans: "CRS=SS."

CRS behavior was complemented by two other groups: the Occident and the civic action committees. The former, a well-armed neofascist group, mounted commando attacks against the students. At one point, it invaded a portion of the Sorbonne, spreading fright and anxiety throughout the Latin Quarter. Its terrorist acts helped mobilize even the apathetic students, such as those in medicine.

The civic action committees—in fact, vigilante groups —were organized throughout France after de Gaulle's May 30 address. Frequently armed, the committees operated through June, disrupting the campaigns of opposition candidates or visiting violence upon them. The committees were particularly harsh on Communist candidates and their supporters.

On the whole, the May revolution was comparatively non-violent, considering the magnitude and duration of the upheaval. Injuries were common on all sides, of course, and some destruction of property is well documented, but only a handful of fatalities have been reported.

THE INTERNATIONAL SITUATION

Student movements are necessarily international if for no other reason than they are ignited and powerfully nourished by anti-capitalism and anti-imperialism. Student movements everywhere speak a common language in opposing the bureaucratization of neocapitalist society, its interventions in the Algerias and Vietnams, and in some cases its implicit or explicit racist policies. In particular, they have seen the Vietnam struggle as a trial of strength between imperialism and the revolutionary forces of the Third World.

The French revolutionaries were quite conscious of the international character of the May struggle and they consciously sought international support. Wrote Cohn-Bendit, "Revolution as well as counterrevolution are international, and much as the student movements in Spain, America, Japan, Italy, et cetera influenced the French student movement, so the French student movement . . . can serve as an example elsewhere."[75] He maintained that the March 22 Movement was organized in part as an expression of support for the actions of the German SDS against the Springer publishing empire. An analogous point of view is expressed by Jacques Sauvageot: "I believe that events outside found an echo here in France. Besides, student movements are inevitably international, and the French movement is sensitive to anything that happens in any university anywhere in the world."[76]

International support for the revolutionaries was quite pervasive. Organizations and groups similar to those active in France in 1968 sprang up in nearly all Western and many Eastern countries. On May 9, 1968, representatives from leftist groups in Belgium, Italy, the Netherlands, Spain, West Germany, and elsewhere met in Paris to declare solidarity with the French revolutionaries and extend moral and material support. At that meeting a decision was reached to expand the struggle of the students into a struggle of the working class.

This spillover from the university into the factory is a unique feature of the May revolution. Through it, the revolutionaries hoped to establish unity with the working class at home and abroad, and especially to reach the exploited peoples of the Third World. Said Sauvageot, "The factory struggle has an international character; capitalist countries are linked together, as are all movements directed against them. . . . We are not content to express solidarity with the struggles pursued in such and such a country, we carry the same struggle to every country. . . . Our solidarity with the struggles in the Third World cannot be overemphasized."[77] Student/worker unity, in short, is a means for confronting the neocapitalist society at home and abroad and supporting the revolutionary struggles of the peoples of the Third World.

Although there was much spiritual, moral, and ideological support for the May revolutionaries at the international level, the extent of actual material support is unknown. The French authorities suggested that the government had proof of foreign finances and supplies provided to the revolutionaries, and they hinted at the influence of an international Maoist conspiracy controlled from Peking. Overt links are difficult to identify, however, although the Maoist regime devoted considerable coverage to the May revolution and provided much ideological inspiration. Thus, for example: "Although mountains and oceans stand between Paris and Peking, the struggle of the French people is close to our hearts."[78]

In response to an interviewer's question as to whether the French revolutionaries had received support from Communist China, the CIA, or Israel, Cohn-Bendit denied that the March 22 Movement had been a recipient of Chinese assistance, though he believed that "it would not be surprising" if the pro-Chinese groups had received such support. As for the other two, he stated, "it does seem that the CIA has been interested lately: some U.S. newspapers and associations, affiliates or intermediaries of the CIA, have offered us considerable sums; I need not tell you what sort of welcome they receive. As to the Zionists, they are no friends of ours. We are opposed to all imperialisms, including Zionist imperialism. We condemn Israel's nationalism and her expansionist claims."[79]

The French authorities made a concerted effort to discourage international support for the May revolution. They pictured the students as foreign subversives; they stopped busloads of German students at Strasbourg; they were seen checking foreign license plates in the Latin Quarter during the revolution; and they refused Cohn-Bendit a re-entry visa when he returned from a speaking engagement in Germany, obliging him to re-enter illegally. However, the Gaullist regime did not succeed in stemming international support for the French Revolution of May 1968.

SUMMARY

Beginning as a student protest, the French Revolution of
May 1968 rapidly picked up momentum to become a full-
scale political movement aiming at the overthrow of the
Gaullist regime and the transformation of French society.
In retrospect the revolutionaries thought that the Gaullist
regime could have been toppled had they succeeded in
capturing key ministries and public buildings, had the general strike lasted longer, or had the CGT and the PCF not
betrayed the revolution. Why did such an initially promising movement fail?

The May revolution was led by a group of intellectuals
who disagreed on the importance of leadership and its relation to spontaneity. The central notion that an ad hoc
"active minority" can detonate a revolutionary struggle
without attempting to direct and control it is a bit of romanticism fatal to effective revolutionary action. It suggests that there is a built-in momentum to revolutionary
struggle—a notion without much of a foundation in reality.
Revolution creates disorder, to be sure, but this disorder
must be manipulated and turned against the established
regime.

The strength of the ideology of May lies in the universal language that it spoke, a language familiar to leftist
movements the world over. Its underlying humanist, egalitarian, libertarian, and romantic thrust was also a source
of great appeal. On the other hand, its apparent contempt
for reason and planning and its unnecessary glorification of
emotion and spontaneity seriously detracted from its viabil-
ity. Moreover, there was too much ideological purism on
the part of each leader and group, too little conscious effort
to dilute revolutionary ideology to broaden its appeal.

Although some of the French revolutionaries openly
challenged the importance of organization, what they in
fact challenged was not organization as such, but old-style
organization, which, imposed from above, stifles spontaneity. The plethora of organizations without a central co-

ordinating unit, together with factionalism, division, and interorganizational rivalry, seriously hampered revolutionary activity. The solid opposition of the trade unions and the parties of the left, especially the CGT and the PCF, was probably of decisive consequence.

The French revolutionaries lacked anything even faintly resembling a military organization. Even if they had possessed such an apparatus, however, it is unlikely that they would have been able to prevail over a military establishment fully prepared to intervene on behalf of the Gaullist order (see Chapter 7).

There was too short a time, too little preparation, and too little organization to permit the May revolutionaries to employ terror and violence on a conscious and planned basis. Although the revolutionaries received considerable spiritual and moral support on the international level, little or no material assistance was forthcoming.

The May revolution crystallized the fragility—though perhaps temporary—of advanced industrial societies. However, the supreme irony of the May revolution is that, even if the government of de Gaulle had fallen, the student revolutionaries were in no position to assume power. To this topic we shall return in Chapter 7.

Part III

SYNTHESIS

Chapter 7

CONCLUSION

We have set forth a conception of strategy, and we have applied it to the Bolivian, Vietminh, and French revolutions. It remains to pull together the two major parts of the book by scrutinizing the conception of strategy in light of the data from these three revolutions. It remains also to examine the prospects for political revolution in advanced industrial societies—a key issue raised by the French Revolution of 1968.

CONDITIONS

The conditions of political revolution are multiple and complex. Many economic, psychological, social, political, and other changes converge before a revolutionary movement gains momentum.

Important conceptualizations of revolutionary conditions have been advanced by Crane Brinton, James C. Davies, Harry Eckstein, Ivo K. and Rosalind L. Feierabend, Ted Robert Gurr, Chalmers Johnson, George S. Pettee, and Raymond Tanter and Manus Midlarsky. The most useful of these conceptualizations appears to be Gurr's theory of relative deprivation, according to which men's perception of the discrepancy between their aspiration and achievement is the basic condition of all violent behavior. However, according to Gurr, whether relative deprivation actually results in revolutionary violence is a function of both normative and utilitarian justifications for violence and the relative institutional and coercive capabilities of the contending parties.

Our examination, in the foregoing chapters, of the three revolutions suggests that relative deprivation, though fundamentally psychological, may have a variety of bases. While relative deprivation had an economic foundation of varying importance in our three political revolutions, it clearly entailed much more. In Bolivia, the social and political injustices willfully visited upon the Indians (some 85 per cent of the population), as well as the sociopolitical disintegration set in motion by the Chaco War, played pivotal roles in drawing the peasants, the miners, and the urban middle class into revolutionary action. In Vietnam, as John T. McAlister, Jr., concludes, the denial of political power to the native intelligentsia—who had come to expect a measure of political influence commensurate with their newly acquired socioeconomic status —was a basic cause of revolutionary discontent. In France, the archaic character of the educational system, the authoritarianism with which universities and factories were run, and the olympian intransigence of de Gaulle's political rule were among the fundamental causes of the May revolution. All three revolutions combined a desire for material welfare with a quest for liberty, equality, and justice. The French student radicals stressed almost exclusively non-material values.

In all three revolutions there was a process of politicization in which the revolutionaries became aware of, and sought to transcend, what was in one way or another second-class status. The urban intellectuals played the key part in all three revolutions. In Bolivia they received crucial support from the miners; in Vietnam, from the peasantry; and in France, from the young workers.

All three political revolutions exploded in response to identifiable precipitants. In Bolivia the precipitant was the Chaco War; in Vietnam, the French reassertion of control after World War II; and in France, the massive intervention of the police in a student revolt.

STRATEGY

Leadership

While the Bolivian and Vietminh revolutionaries were quite insistent on the need for leadership, the French radicals of 1968 were divided on the issue. Some flatly rejected leadership in favor of spontaneity; others called for an "active minority" to detonate the struggle without attempting to direct it; still others sought to combine spontaneity and leadership. Those who insisted on spontaneity did not consistently view it as unplanned, unengineered action. In one place, for example, Daniel Cohn-Bendit defined "spontaneous" simply as "without official blessing."[1] The French revolutionaries' desire to deny the role of leadership is attributable to two principal considerations: (1) their intense distaste for traditional Communist teachings on the role of a vanguard party, and (2) their sheer inability to control the events they had set in motion. In any case, all three revolutions were in part planned and in part spontaneous, with the Vietminh as the most planned, the French as the most spontaneous, and the Bolivian falling somewhere in between but far closer to the Vietminh than to the French.

Eric Hoffer, as we have seen in Chapter 3, identifies three types of revolutionary leaders in successive stages of revolution: the men of words, the fanatics, and the practical men of action. He believes that if the three roles are played by the same person(s) throughout, the movement is likely to fail. Our findings do not sustain Hoffer's views. To be sure, the men of words and the men of action were present in Bolivia, Vietnam, and France. But the fanatic—who for Hoffer is the key to any revolution—was not universally present, by any stretch of the imagination. Of all the revolutionaries we have considered in the foregoing pages, only Ho Chi Minh and some of his associates can conceivably be labeled "fanatic." The Bolivian and French revolutionaries do not meet the criteria of fanaticism specified by Hoffer. In general, though there was considerable charisma in the leaders of all three revolutions, charisma and fanaticism are not one and the same. Revolutions, it appears, are not the work of fanatics but of more or less "normal" people.

The paucity of empirical data on the social backgrounds of revolutionary leaders does not permit a full-scale analysis. The available data, incorporated into a composite profile of the leaders of the Bolivian, Vietminh, and French revolutions, are presented in Table 7.1.

As the table indicates, the mean age for revolutionary leaders is the mid-thirties. The average age of twenty-six for the French revolutionaries may indicate a tendency toward younger revolutionary leadership in the closing decades of the twentieth century.

Firm generalizations about the geographic origin of revolutionary leaders do not appear warranted. We may note, however, that in contrast to the predominantly urban background of the Bolivian and French revolutionaries, the Vietminh leaders came almost exclusively from rural areas. It would seem, moreover, that regardless of geographic origin, early involvement in national politics in urban areas is a uniform pattern in the development of revolutionary elites. Revolutionary leaders are ordinarily indigenous to the country in which they operate, Che Guevara's adventure in Bolivia being an obvious exception.

The picture is quite clear on the question of social origin: revolutionary leaders are overwhelmingly middle class, with a sprinkling of upper and lower classes. Revolutionary leaders appear to have had moderate exposure to foreign cultures. This is probably determined in large measure by their educational attainment, which turns out to be quite high. As far as occupation is concerned, intellectuals and professionals continue to be in the forefront of revolutionary movements. By virtue of their education and attainment, middle-class intellectuals are among the first to become politically conscious, discover their second-class status, and set out to transform the social order. The emergence of student revolutionary leaders was of course a global trend of the 1960s.

TABLE 7.1

COMPOSITE PROFILE OF REVOLUTIONARY LEADERS

Characteristic	Bolivian Leaders	Vietminh Leaders	French Leaders
Average age at the time of revolution	39.3	41.4	26
Place of birth	No uniformity	Cent. & So. Vietnam	No apparent uniformity
Social origin	No uniformity (upper, middle, lower)	Middle class (largely rural)	Overwhelmingly middle class
Occupation	Professional Labor leader Politician	Professional Laborer	Professional Student
Education	Very high (except Lechin)	Comparatively high	Exceptionally high
Foreign exposure	Moderate	Moderate	Moderate

In short, while the leaders of the French Revolution of 1968 were much younger and better educated than the others, the available data indicate that the Bolivian, Vietminh, and French revolutionaries had much in common with their counterparts elsewhere (see Chapter 3).

Ideology

All three political revolutions employed value-laden, action-related systems of beliefs and ideas to legitimize their demands, mobilize and politicize the masses, challenge the existing regime, and bring about a new social order. The Bolivian and Vietminh revolutions employed indigenous and eclectic ideologies. Both ideologies drew upon foreign sources, to be sure, but the revolutionaries carefully adapted foreign ideas to the needs of their respective countries. The May revolution, on the other hand, fashioned an ideology consciously and explicitly international, relying upon the experience of student revolts around the world.

In all three political revolutions the Marxist ideology played a role, most prominently in Vietnam and least prominently in Bolivia. The case of France represents a special blend of the ideologies of Marxism, anarchism, romanticism, and classic democracy.

Nationalism played a definite part in both the Bolivian and the Vietminh revolutions. There is a crucial distinction, however. Bolivian nationalism was directed primarily toward social integration, economic development, political and economic equality, and the elimination of foreign business influence. By contrast, Vietminh nationalism was directed primarily at the expulsion of the French colonialists. Anti-imperialism emerged as a dominant force in Vietnam, because it blended well with nationalism and fitted closely the conditions of the country.

Anti-imperialism played a powerful role in the French Revolution of 1968 as well, but in an entirely different sense. Speaking the universal language of student revolt, the French revolutionaries denounced in principle the exploitation of the Third World by the advanced countries of the West—a denunciation equally applicable to their own country. Anti-nationalist in outlook, they proposed to replace the exploitative neocapitalist society with a community of self-management, direct democracy, freedom, self-expression, and spontaneity.

A degree of romanticism is endemic in all revolutionary ideologies, since revolution entails the struggle of the oppressed against the oppressor, the search of the downtrodden for a better, more humane society. But if the struggle is to succeed, revolutionary romanticism must not be permitted to befuddle realities or to obscure possibilities. A basic weakness of the ideology of May was its total contempt for reason and its unqualified glorification of emotion, action, and spontaneity. The French revolutionaries claimed to have reversed the relationship between theory and action: action, they insisted, must always precede theory. They overlooked the point, however, that, unguided by theory, action is likely to falter and consume itself.

The dilution of ideology was an unmistakable characteristic of the Bolivian and Vietminh revolutions, but not of the French. The MNR leaders, rather than dismissing fascism-Nazism-communism outright, manipulated these ideologies to their own advantage until after the seizure of political power in 1952. The same opportunism was characteristic of the Vietminh leaders, who made a concerted effort to soft-pedal the Marixt-Leninist ideology in order to maximize support at home and abroad. By contrast, the May revolutionaries were constrained by ideological purism. Partly for this reason and partly due to the presence of a multiplicity of leaders and groups, the French revolutionaries did not seem readily able to maneuver and compromise.

Organization

All three political revolutions employed organizations of varying type and effectiveness. This is true even of the French revolutionaries, who, venerating spontaneity, openly challenged the need for organization. On balance, however, what they opposed was not organization as such, but old-style organization—for example, of the Communist variety.

The most sophisticated organizational apparatus—both political and military—was encountered in Vietnam, and the least sophisticated in France. The Bolivians were well organized politically but they lacked an elaborate military apparatus, a disadvantage they offset at a crucial juncture by using the forces of the regime against itself. The Vietminh Revolution was led by a traditional Marxist-Leninist party, the Bolivian by an amorphous moderate/leftist party, and the French, lacking a political party as such, by an assortment of Marxist, Trotskyite, Maoist, and anarchist groups. The Vietminh and Bolivian parties were small and elitist; the French groups, though they claimed to be mass, were also run by elites. The Vietminh and Bolivian parties were tightly organized and well disciplined; the French groups were neither.

The revolutionary organization in Bolivia initially relied almost exclusively on party politics. Having found parliamentarianism to be of no avail, the MNR turned to military action. As military tactics proved insufficient, it combined political and military activity in a quest to remake Bolivia socially, politically, and economically.

Relying heavily on the Chinese experience, the Vietminh revolutionaries sought from the beginning to fuse political and military activity. Applying the teachings of Mao Tsetung to the circumstances of Vietnam, the Vietminh developed a host of political/military doctrines for fighting the French. Mao's ideas of protracted conflict based on peasant guerrilla warfare proved particularly suitable to the conditions of the country. The Vietminh created an extensive human network for gathering intelligence, disseminating propaganda, and mobilizing and politicizing the masses. The chief military departure from the Chinese experience was highlighted in the battle of Dien Bien Phu: if successful, a decisive military engagement will create repercussions—political, military, and psychological—that help shorten a protracted struggle.

The French revolutionaries relied on a plethora of political groups but no military organizations whatever. Cohn-Bendit attempted to make a virtue of this when he boasted, "It has been said, and rightly so, that for the first time in history a revolution could have been made without recourse to arms."[2] The multiplicity of organizations without a directing center hampered effective action. Factionalism, division, and interorganizational rivalry were rampant. There was no viable political apparatus to counter the solid opposition of the established parties.

Recognizing that all military activity is guided by political objectives, military thinkers of all persuasions have traditionally subjected the military organization to close political suupervision and control. Similarly, following the teachings of Mao, the Vietminh revolutionaries asserted the supremacy of the party over the army. In Bolivia, too, to the extent to which a military apparatus existed, it was held subservient to politics.

In recent times, this view has been flatly challenged by some revolutionaries, particularly those associated with the Cuban experience. Fidel Castro, Che Guevara, and Régis Debray have all attempted to reverse the relationship between the party and the army in the Latin American context.[3] Debray, who is most systematic on this point, argues forcefully that the Cuban experience demonstrates that revolution in Latin America cannot follow the pattern established by other revolutions. The Cuban revolution is a "revolution in the revolution," different from all revolutions that preceded it. In particular, he maintains, the foremost task throughout revolution is not organization and politicization of the masses but the consolidation of military strength.

Just as Mao and Giap modified Lenin's theories to fit the conditions of China and Vietnam, it is Debray's contention that Castro had to modify the theories of Mao and Giap to fit Cuba. The Cuban example is a direct reversal of Mao's dictum that, although "Political power grows out of the barrel of a gun," under all conditions it is "the Party [that] commands the gun, and the gun must never be allowed to command the Party."[4] Successful revolutionary activity in Latin America requires the opposite practice:

the political apparatus must be controlled by the military. While the success of the revolution lies in the realization that guerrilla warfare is essentially political, the party and the guerrilla must become one and the same, with the guerrilla in command. The guerrilla cannot tolerate a duality of functions and powers, but must become the political as well as the military vanguard of the people. *"The guerrilla is the party in embryo."*[5] This union of Marxist theory and new revolutionary practice is the novelty of the Cuban Revolution, says Debray. The armed destruction of the enemy—the public demonstration of his fallibility—is the most effective propaganda for the local population. Consequently, in Latin America today, the chief concern must be the development of guerrilla units (*focos*) and not the strengthening of political parties.[6]

A strikingly similar analysis in a different context has been offered by Nathan Leites and Charles Wolf, Jr., who stress the unqualified importance of organization in insurgency. In effect, they argue that organization is important enough to create public support—or indeed to serve as a substitute for public support. An insurgency movement, they believe, *"need not* initially have the spontaneous support, sympathy, or loyalty of the people, not even of a significant minority of the people, although it may in fact enjoy such support. . . . Thorough organization and effective coercion can enjoin or engender particular modes of behavior by the population. . . ."[7] The crucial task in insurgency is not mobilization of popular support but careful organization, effective use of force, and utilization of an effective intelligence system.

Che Guevara's failure in Bolivia indicates weaknesses in the Cuban revolutionary strategy as conceptualized by Debray and others. It also calls into question the thesis put forward by Leites and Wolf. The Bolivian adventure of 1966–67 demonstrates that, however dedicated it may be to proclaimed values of freedom and humanity, a small guerrilla force in an unfamiliar and hostile environment, isolated from a distrustful local population whose language it does not speak, and relentlessly pursued by a superior government force equipped with an array of modern counterguerrilla techniques, is doomed to fail. It is also worth remembering in this regard that Debray and others probably misinterpreted the Cuban revolutionary experience to assert the supremacy of the military over the political and to advance the argument that Castro's guerrilla *focos* had played an exclusive part in creating a revolutionary situation. In truth, however, such a situation existed to a large extent prior to the emergence of the *focos*.

Terror and Violence

The purpose of the discussion of terror and violence throughout this book has been to come to terms with the essential dimensions of revolutionary activity. Revolutions are necessarily messy affairs; they involve the use of terror and violence by both the insurgents and the incumbents. Revolutionary terror is used primarily to undermine enemy morale and to create an atmosphere of uncertainty, anxiety, and despair. It is also employed as a means of provoking governmental terror, which everywhere has turned the population against the existing regime.

The most extensive use of terror and violence took place in the Vietminh Revolution, as both sides relied on force to advance their objectives. The French devised a systematic and often indiscriminate policy of eliminating their Vietnamese opponents—whether nationalist or Communist—a policy that helped alienate the people. The Vietminh, with major exceptions, as we have seen, relied on a purposeful and effective policy of terror and violence to further their aims. They used terror as a means of highlighting the vulnerability of the French and of proselytizing among the non-French members of the French forces. On some occasions, the Vietminh undermined their own popularity by launching unnecessary purges and violence against the general population.

The Bolivian leaders consciously shied away from the indiscriminate employment of terror and violence. The MNR did imprison or exile its political opponents, but it did not undertake wholesale purges of the Bolivian people.

Throughout the prerevolutionary period, the MNR leaders adopted a sophisticated policy of inviting governmental terror, which helped mobilize the masses to support the MNR. A principal reason for the MNR's relative lack of reliance on terror and violence was that it was a well-established and institutionalized political party fully aware of its goals and objectives and enjoying considerable public confidence.

While the French revolutionaries succeeded in provoking the government to adopt a policy of systematic terror against the insurgents, the use of terror as a conscious means of implementing revolutionary objectives was virtually non-existent in the May revolution. Events unfolded with extreme rapidity; few revolutionaries had anticipated the scope of the struggle; few had time to plan; few had the necessary implements for launching terror. In the closing phase of the struggle, the revolutionaries did undertake terrorist activity in the Latin Quarter, but as Thomas P. Thornton points out, "terror in late stages of an insurrectionary movement can look very much like (and frequently is) the irrational death throes of the movement."[8]

The experience of the three revolutions considered above does not cast a definitive light on the role of revolutionary terror in the strategy of political revolution. It does bring out, however, a uniform trend in which the initiation of governmental terror helped undermine the government's effectiveness and legitimacy and caused large segments of the population to identify with the revolutionaries. It also shows that the extent to which revolutionary terror is undertaken against the general population is a function of the degree to which the revolutionary party is institutionalized and capable of mobilizing the masses. Where such a party does exist, and a high degree of mobilization has taken place, terror will tend to be minimal and purposeful. Where such a party does not exist, and mobilization has not taken place, the masses will be difficult to organize, and terror will tend to be high and at times directionless. In either case, terrorist activity against the incumbent regime may continue to be quite extensive.

The International Situation

All three political revolutions were directly affected by international forces. The Bolivian revolutionaries were well aware of the international implications of a revolution in Bolivia. In an effort to neutralize support for the opposition and capture support for themselves, the MNR leaders diluted their ideological posture and took stances complimentary to those of the United States and Argentina. Paz Estenssoro in particular did much to capture the good will of the international community and to convince the United States that the nationalist/leftist MNR offered the most viable alternative for Bolivia.

The Vietminh demonstrated an acute consciousness of international forces and the importance of capturing foreign allies and assistance. On numerous occasions, the Vietminh revolutionaries soft-pedaled the Communist ideology in order to maximize popular appeal at home and abroad, avoid alienating non-Communist powers, and capture new friends. When dealing with the United States they consistently appealed to key principles of Western democracy. The victory of the Communists in China brought the Vietminh much material and spiritual support. The Chinese provided the Vietnamese Communists with arms, ammunition, and supplies, as well as secure base areas inside China.

The May revolutionaries took pride in the international character of the movement they had launched, and deliberately sought foreign assistance. The student movements being international, support for the May revolutionaries was automatic and pervasive. Through such support, the revolutionaries hoped to confront the neocapitalist society at home and abroad. Although the French radicals received considerable moral, spiritual, and ideological support, the extent of actual material assistance appears negligible.

In two important ways international support for the French revolutionaries differed from similar support accorded Bolivia and Vietnam. First, international support came exclusively from like-minded student and leftist groups, not from any formally organized government. By the same token, this support was not of a kind to have a decisive bearing on the course of events in the May revolution. The government of Charles de Gaulle was in a far better position to influence and control international forces. Nevertheless, in all three political revolutions the manipulation of the international situation played an important role and demonstrated the close interplay between domestic and international politics.

Conclusion

The conception of strategy developed in this book appears to hold a fundamental validity. Political revolutions are successful to the extent to which the revolutionaries are capable of employing and manipulating the components of strategy in the context of a particular time, place, and set of conditions. It seems equally clear, however, that the degree to which the various components are in fact present varies from revolution to revolution. Thus, for example, the use of terror and violence was relatively high in Vietnam and relatively low in Bolivia. Similarly, revolutionary organization was highly sophisticated in Vietnam and far less so in France. Since each revolution unfolds in a more or less unique set of circumstances, it must rely on its own unique "mix" among the components of strategy.

While not all the components of strategy are equally involved in every revolution, collectively they seem to do a good job of gauging the potential success or failure of revolutionary movements. A primary value of the analysis presented in this book is that it narrows the complex topic of revolutionary strategy to a series of concrete and operational components. Further applications of the concept of strategy to other revolutions—and the delineation of the "laws" governing the "mix" among the components—constitute promising next steps for empirical inquiry.

PROSPECTS

A Successful Revolution in France?

While Che Guevara still reigned supreme in Cuba, a group of youthful radicals from the United States visited him to express admiration for his unrelenting struggle against American imperialism. In return, Guevara reportedly expressed envy for the young radicals, for, he said, *they* were the ones who had the unique opportunity to take on imperialism on its own home ground. He admonished the young revolutionaries to approach this task with utmost seriousness.[9]

Ever since this exchange, the prospects for political revolution in advanced industrial societies have taken on an increasing reality in the minds of some revolutionary groups. The French upheaval of 1968 added what seemed like fresh credibility to this image and directly focused attention on the possibility of bringing about a political revolution in neocapitalist countries.

Specifically, a number of writers have advanced two major propositions: (1) the May revolution could have succeeded, and (2) the experience of France can be duplicated in other advanced industrial societies. As we have seen in Chapter 6, for example, Daniel Cohn-Bendit has argued that the May revolution could have borne fruit had the revolutionaries captured some of the key ministries, had the general strike lasted longer, or had the Communist Party not betrayed its historic mission. "The events in France," he writes, "have proved that revolution is possible in even a highly industrialized capitalist society. Those who argued that the working class had outgrown revolution stood convicted of theoretical and practical incompetence, a fact that suggests it is high time to discover why the working class has remained so passive for so long." He asserted that "small revolutionary groups can, at the right time and place, rupture the system decisively and irreversibly."[10]

The May revolutionaries did bring out the (temporary) vulnerability and fragility of highly developed societies, to be sure, but these and similar arguments overlook some key points on the possibility of a successful revolution in 1968 France. For one thing, the revolutionaries would have had no opportunity to capture any ministries, for, apparently unknown to Cohn-Bendit, all public buildings were being heavily guarded by the military and the police. Moreover, the French military had not even begun to intervene publicly, and there is every likelihood that it would have done so—at least up to a point. Indeed, in his May 29 secret consultations with French military commanders at home and abroad, de Gaulle clearly contemplated even the use of the seventy thousand French troops stationed in Germany. Finally, even if the Gaullist regime had collapsed, the May revolutionaries would have been in no position to capture power or to implement their programs. They had no experienced group of leaders, no effective organization, no preparation to assume political office. The most that can be said is that, had de Gaulle fallen, he would have been replaced by a coalition government of the Socialists and Communists, both of whom the May revolutionaries despised.

Some have argued that the May revolution in fact succeeded, because the government of de Gaulle did fall, at least indirectly, in the streets of Paris. The replacement of a Charles de Gaulle by a Georges Pompidou hardly qualifies as a political revolution, however.

Revolution in America?

Can the experience of France be duplicated in other advanced industrial societies? In particular, can there be a political revolution in the United States?

One way of exploring this question in some depth is to consider the conditions in contemporary America that may favor political revolution and the conditions that may hamper it, in an effort to arrive at an appraisal of the over-all revolutionary potential in the United States today.

Conditions Favoring Revolution. Two conditions in the contemporary United States would seem conducive to revolution. One is considerable disaffection among students and intellectuals on the issues of race, poverty, militarism, and war. Though there is much protest, moral outrage, and demand for justice, however, the net effect cannot be considered a disintegration of the prevailing ideology or a desertion of the intellectuals, for large segments of the population continue to side with the ruling regime—whether Democratic or Republican. To be sure, the protesters have succeeded in their objective of exposing the hypocrisy and authoritarianism of the Establishment, but countless illustrations document the irony that the Establishment and the "silent majority" are not particularly perturbed by hypocrisy or authoritarianism.

The second condition has to do with the tradition—indeed, the institutionalization—of violence in American society. Up until the 1960s there was much mythology about the absence of violence in the United States. However, an array of recent studies—particularly those of the National Commission on the Causes and Prevention of Violence[11]—have exploded this myth and have graphically documented the extent of violence in the American past as well as the American present. Particularly impressive in this regard is the work of Ted Robert Gurr. His comparative study of violence in 114 countries showed, for example, that in the 1960s there was proportionally more collective violence in the United States than in most other countries. He found specifically that (1) as compared with the other 113 countries, the United States ranked twenty-fourth in the total magnitude (amount) of violence and sixth in the magnitude of turmoil (demonstrations and riots), and (2) as compared with the seventeen other democratic countries of Western Europe and the British Commonwealth, the United States ranked first in the total magnitude of violence.[12] On the basis of this and similar findings, another scholar has concluded:

We must recognize that, despite our pious official disclaimers, we have always operated with a heavy de-

pendence upon violence in even our highest and most
idealistic endeavors. We must take stock of what we
have done rather than what we have said. When that
is done, the realization that we have been an incor-
rigibly violent people is overwhelming. We must realize that violence has not been the action only of the
roughnecks and racists among us but has been the
tactic of the most upright and respected of our
people.[13]

To document the pervasiveness of violence in the United
States is not to say that the American people are inherently
or biologically more violent than any other. It is to say that
there have been certain conditions in the American past
and the American present that are conducive to violent
behavior.

In so far as the historical setting is concerned, to rely on
the work of the Commission on Violence, the American
past is a laboratory for the "celebration of violence in
good causes."[14] In this connection, one need only consider the revolutionary doctrine underlying the Declaration
of Independence and the Jeffersonian advocacy of violent
overthrow of an illegitimate government, as well as the
pervasive violence associated with the American Revolution, the Civil War, the Mexican War, the Spanish-
American War, and all America's other wars. Moreover,
the westward movement engendered an aggressive philosophy of each-man-for-himself and generated violence—violence visited by the white man upon the Indian, by the
white man upon the black man, and by the white man
upon the white man. The encounter with the frontier, as
one scholar has pointed out, was "an invitation to violence."[15] Finally urbanization and industrialization proceeded with such rapidity in America as to create widespread dislocation, frustration, and discontent. One need
only recall the labor violence of the nineteenth and
twentieth centuries.[16]

As far as the current situation is concerned, two considerations are particularly relevant. First, intense relative deprivation continues to be a fact of life in the United States.
The struggle of minority groups—the Indians, the Blacks,

the Chicanos, the Puerto Ricans—for recognition and achievement continues. This struggle coincides with a general and persistent coexistence of affluence and poverty—a disjunction cutting across racial and cultural lines and affecting all segments of the population.

A second consideration relates to cultural conditioning. From his earliest exposures to the American culture, the individual is confronted with and conditioned to violence —violence in the press, in television, in sports, in comic strips, and even in toys (as sophisticated replicas of weapons of warfare).[17] Violence becomes institutionalized and accepted as an ordinary, routine, natural mode of behavior. General David M. Shoup, former Commandant of the Marine Corps, has gone so far as to say, "To many Americans, military training, expeditionary service, and warfare are merely extensions of the entertainment and games of childhood."[18]

In a word, there has been much violence in America, but violence is not the same as revolution. It is, as we have seen, only one of several ingredients.

Conditions Hindering Revolution. An impressive array of conditions converge to frustrate political revolution in the United States in the foreseeable future. To begin with, the popular attitude toward revolution is totally negative. Whereas in France the term "revolution" continues to carry a special romantic appeal,[19] as it once did in the United States, in America today revolution is seen as an aberration, a pathological condition that afflicts a few wicked men outside the mainstream of popular consciousness. The central concern is with measures to neutralize potential radicals, stabilize the situation, and maintain "law and order."

Some of the reasons for this change of American attitude are not difficult to identify. In the twentieth century, revolution has been associated with the Communist countries; one might even say that an American fear of Communist revolution has been generalized into a phobia against all revolutions. Moreover, the substantial majority of the population is generally content with things as they are. A process of *embourgeoisement* of the lower classes has proceeded to a point of nearly turning the entire country into a vast spiritual middle class. It may be, as Herbert Marcuse has pointed out, that the social classes have been duped into a condition of "false consciousness"[20] (note the subtle play on Marx and Engels), but that is entirely beside the point. The dominant majority—which includes the working class—is eminently satisfied, even reactionary, false consciousness notwithstanding.

A second condition hindering political revolution in the United States today is the absence of a comprehensive and integrative revolutionary ideology to appeal to, mobilize, and unite the discontented elements of the population. While it is true that one can probably develop for the United States a composite profile of a revolutionary ideology similar to the one we developed for France, such an exercise would have only an intellectual reality, while the effectiveness of the resultant ideology would be undermined by dissension, factionalism, rivalry, and lack of organization and co-ordination among the would-be revolutionary groups.

A third consideration is the exemplary efficiency of the ruling regime. The ruling authorities—whether Democratic or Republican—have been in total command of the situation. They have repeatedly demonstrated their ability and willingness to use force decisively, as witness, for example, the treatment of the Weathermen and the Black Panther Party. The coercive potential of the Establishment has been greatly facilitated by modern technology, not only in terms of the availability of new weapons and techniques, but also in the perfection of a highly sophisticated intelligence system. It is also noteworthy that large segments of the American population consider the employment of governmental coercion as legitimate and necessary, as witness, for example, the positive response to Mayor Richard Daley's handling of the events surrounding the 1968 Democratic National Convention in Chicago.

A fourth condition deals with the predominantly urban character of the country. In urban industrial societies temporary disruptions are possible but political revolutions are unlikely. In contrast to the isolated rural areas of China, Vietnam, Cuba, and Bolivia, the urban industrial societies are under minute control of the military and the police and are virtually impervious to prolonged revolutionary disruption. The experience of France would seem to support this proposition.

Attention recently has been devoted to the possible emergence of urban guerrillas and the operationalization of urban guerrilla warfare. Relying on the experience of Cuba and France one writer has advocated, for example, the development of "action committees" patterned after the Cuban *focos* as a means of initiating revolutionary insurrection in advanced industrial societies. Since in such societies "the scientific revolution has created a limited number of vital nerve centers," these centers can be easily paralyzed. He writes:

> Like the Cuban *focos* the action committees try to create an explosive situation by setting off simultaneous sparks in industrial centers throughout the country. We will attempt to build *focos* of extraparliamentary political activity and mass violence against the system. Our aim is to polarize the social forces to such an extent that the finely-balanced social fabric will be destroyed and those who destroy will, in a parallel movement, construct the new society.[21]

If by urban guerrilla warfare is meant random hit-and-run tactics—ambushing and assaulting the police, sabotaging and bombing public buildings, kidnapping various symbols of authority—such activities could hardly constitute an effective strategy for toppling a modern government. If, on the other hand, by urban guerrilla warfare is meant a sustained and meaningful political-military-psychological offensive against the authorities, it is doomed to failure for reasons discussed above. What the writer of the above passage seems to overlook is the efficiency of a modern intelligence system that would prevent such insurrectionary forces from emerging, as well as the power of a military/police apparatus that would handily crush them if they did emerge. The most likely outcome of urban guerrilla warfare in advanced societies is a wave of repression readily launched and conveniently justified by the political authorities and the silent majorities on whom they rely.[22]

A final condition hampering political revolution in the United States today is the pluralistic character of the country.[23] Social, political, and economic pluralism means that power and authority are diffuse, dispersed, and fragmented. In contrast to the rigid centralization of French society, in which a successful assault upon a dozen key ministries *might* topple the government, the United States is far less vulnerable, because power and authority are shared by numerous groups, organizations, parties, and governments at the municipal, county, state, and national levels. In such unitary societies as Ethiopia, Portugal, Spain, and Taiwan, the task of revolution is simplified because of the single center of authority that needs to be smashed. In multicentered countries, by contrast, the situation is entirely different. Such societies have the further advantage of affording the population a sense of satisfaction associated with political participation, involvement, and decision making at various levels of government. It is of course true that participation may be illusory, but that is beside the point; a sense of efficacy derives simply from a belief in (not the reality of) participation. Once the illusion is exposed, however, alienation may well set in.

To recapitulate, available evidence would seem to point to a strongly negative conclusion regarding the possibility of political revolution in the United States in the foreseeable future. In the longer run new forms of revolutionary upheaval may conceivably be spawned, but the potentials and shortcomings of these forms will have to be appraised in due course on their own merit. Revolution, to be sure, is a way of bringing about change, and revolutionary strategy a means of bringing about revolution. Revolution is bound to fail if it lacks a conscious strategy. But strategy is no panacea in itself and cannot be mechanically imposed in a social and political vacuum. Revolutionary strategy has limitations as well as possibilities, and the scrupulous observation of the limitations is as essential as the bold exploitation of the possibilities.

NOTES

PREFACE

1. In the latter group, four names come immediately to mind: Feliks Gross, *The Seizure of Political Power in a Century of Revolutions* (New York: Philosophical Library, 1958), Part III; Samuel P. Huntington, "Patterns of Violence in World Politics," in Huntington, ed., *Changing Patterns of Military Politics* (New York: Free Press, 1962); Chalmers Johnson, *Revolutionary Change* (Boston: Little, Brown & Co., 1966), Chapter 8; and Philip Selznick, *The Organizational Weapon: A Study of Bolshevik Strategy and Tactics* (New York: McGraw-Hill Book Co., 1952). Ted Robert Gurr's *Why Men Rebel* (Princeton, N.J.: Princeton University Press, 1970) contains an implicit discussion of the strategy of violence (though not of political revolution) throughout and an explicit discussion on pp. 352–57. Martin Oppenheimer's *The Urban Guerrilla* (Chicago: Quadrangle Books, 1969) shows considerable awareness of the problems of strategy.

CHAPTER 1

1. See also Brooks Adams, *The Theory of Social Revolutions* (New York: Macmillan Co., 1913); Peter Calvert, *Revolution* (New York: Praeger Publishers, 1970); Calvert, "Revolution: The Politics of Violence," *Political Studies*, 15 (1967), pp. 1–11; Lyford P. Edwards, *The Natural History of Revolution* (Chicago: University of Chicago Press, 1927); Alexander Groth, *Revolution and Elite Access: Some Hypotheses on Aspects of Political Change* (University of California, Davis: Institute of Governmental Affairs, 1966); Rex D. Hopper, "The Revolutionary Process: A Frame of Reference for the Study of Revolutionary Movements," *Social Forces*, 28 (1950), pp. 270–79.

2. Carl J. Friedrich, "An Introductory Note on Revolution," in Friedrich, ed., *Revolution* (New York: Atherton Press, 1967), p. 5.

3. Eugene Kamenka, "The Concept of a Political Revolution," in Friedrich, ed., *Revolution*, p. 124.

4. Raymond Tanter and Manus Midlarsky, "A Theory of Revolution," *Journal of Conflict Resolution*, 11 (1967), p. 267.

5. George S. Pettee, *The Process of Revolution* (New York: Harper & Bros., 1938), p. 3.

6. Paul Schrecker, "Revolution as a Problem in the Philosophy of History," in Friedrich, ed., *Revolution*, p. 38 (italics in original).

7. Hannah Arendt, *On Revolution* (New York: Viking Press, 1963), pp. 2, 21, *et passim*.

8. Ibid., pp. 21–22.

9. Ibid., p. 28.

10. Chalmers Johnson, *Revolution and the Social System* (Stanford University: Hoover Institution on War, Revolution, and Peace, 1964); Johnson, *Revolutionary Change* (Boston: Little, Brown & Co., 1966).

11. Johnson, *Revolution and the Social System*, esp. pp. 12, 22.

12. Johnson, *Revolutionary Change*, esp. pp. 105, 119.

13. Ibid., p. 12.

14. Charles A. Ellwood, "A Psychological Theory of Revolutions," *American Journal of Sociology*, 11 (1905–6), p. 51.

15. Ibid., p. 58.

16. Peter H. Amann, "Revolution: A Redefinition," *Political Science Quarterly*, 77 (1962), p. 38.

17. Gustave Le Bon, *The Psychology of Revolution* (New York: G. P. Putnam's Sons, 1913), p. 24.

18. Dale Yoder, "Current Definitions of Revolution," *American Journal of Sociology*, 32 (1926), p. 441.

19. Cyril E. Black, "Revolution, Modernization, and Communism," in Black, ed., *Communism and Revolution: The Strategic Uses of Political Violence* (Princeton, N.J.: Princeton University Press, 1964), p. 41.

20. *Cf.* Alfred Meusel's conception of revolution as "a sudden and far-reaching change, a major break in the continuity of development. . . . A major change in the political order . . . must be preceded or accompanied by a drastic change in the relations among the different groups and classes in society. Thus a recasting of the social order is, at least in modern times, a far more important characteristic of revolutions than a change of the political constitution or the use of violence in the attainment of this end." Meusel, "Revolution and Counter-Revolution," *Encyclopedia of the Social Sciences*, Vol. 13 (New York: Macmillan Co., 1934), p. 367. Relying on Meusel, Sigmund Neumann has defined revolution as "a sweeping, fundamental change in political organization, social structure, economic property control and the predominant myth of a social order, thus indicating a major break in the continuity of development." Neumann, "The International Civil War," *World Politics*, 1 (1949), p. 333, n. 1. Samuel P. Huntington in a similar vein has approached revolution as "a rapid, fundamental, and violent domestic change in the dominant values and myths of a society, in its political institutions, social structure, leadership, and government activity and policies." Huntington, *Political Order in Changing Societies* (New Haven, Conn.: Yale University Press, 1968), p. 264.

21. *Cf.* Hugh Davis Graham and Ted Robert Gurr, "Introduction," in Graham and Gurr, eds., *Violence in America: Historical and Comparative Perspectives* (New York: Signet Books, 1969), p. xvii; H. L. Nieburg, *Political Violence: The Behavioral Process* (New York: St. Martin's Press, 1969), p. 13; Nieburg, "The Threat of Violence and Social Change," *American Political Science Review*, 56 (December 1962), p. 865.

22. Frantz Fanon, *The Wretched of the Earth* (New York: Grove Press, 1968), pp. 41–42.

23. Ibid., pp. 61, 86.

24. Nieburg, *Political Violence*, p. 5. *Cf.* Lewis A. Coser, *The Functions of Social Conflict* (New York: Free Press, 1956); Coser, "Some Social Functions of Violence," *The Annals*, 364 (March 1966), pp. 8–18; Ted Robert Gurr, *Why Men Rebel* (Princeton, N.J.: Princeton University Press, 1970). The Gurr volume is by far the most comprehensive and provocative study of violence to date.

25. Georges Sorel, *Reflections on Violence* (New York: Collier Books, 1961), p. 50.

26. Nieburg, *Political Violence*, esp. p. 13; Nieburg, "The Threat of Violence and Social Change," esp. p. 865.

27. Fanon, *The Wretched of the Earth*, p. 94.

28. Coser, "Some Social Functions of Violence," *passim*.

29. See, for example, Coser, *The Functions of Social Conflict*; Coser, "Some Social Functions of Violence"; Gurr, *Why Men Rebel*, esp. pp. 210 ff.; Nieburg, *Political Violence*; Nieburg, "The Threat of Violence and Social Change"; Robert C. North, Howard E. Koch, Jr., and Dina A. Zines, "The Integrative Functions of Conflict," *Journal of Conflict Resolution*, 4 (1960), pp. 355–74; E. V. Walter, *Terror and Resistance: A Study of Political Violence* (New York: Oxford University Press, 1969), esp. Chapter 2.

CHAPTER 2

1. Feliks Gross, *The Seizure of Political Power in a Century of Revolutions* (New York: Philosophical Library, 1958), Chapter 3.

2. George S. Pettee, "Revolution—Typology and Process," in Carl J. Friedrich, ed., *Revolution* (New York: Atherton Press, 1967), pp. 15 ff.

3. Raymond Tanter and Manus Midlarsky, "A Theory of Revolution," *Journal of Conflict Resolution*, 11 (1967), pp. 264 ff.

4. Chalmers Johnson, *Revolution and the Social System* (Stanford University: Hoover Institution on War, Revolution, and Peace, 1964), Chapter 2.

5. Harry Eckstein, "On the Etiology of Internal War," *History and Theory*, 4 (1965); reprinted in Eric A. Nordlinger, ed., *Politics and Society: Studies in Comparative Political Sociology* (Englewood Cliffs, N.J.: Prentice-Hall, Inc., 1970), pp. 287–88. *Cf.* Eckstein, "Introduction: Toward the Theoretical Study of Internal War," in

Eckstein, ed., *Internal War: Problems and Approaches* (New York: Free Press, 1964), p. 12.

6. James N. Rosenau, "Internal War as an International Event," in Rosenau, ed., *International Aspects of Civil Strife* (Princeton, N.J.: Princeton University Press, 1964), pp. 60 ff.

7. James H. Meisel, *Counterrevolution: How Revolutions Die* (New York: Atherton Press, 1966), p. 33 *et passim.*

8. *Cf.* Jerome H. Skolnick, *The Politics of Protest* (New York: Ballantine Books, 1969), esp. p. xxvii; George Wada and James C. Davies, "Riots and Rioters," *Western Political Quarterly*, 10 (1957), p. 864.

9. A searching analysis of the concept of coup d'état is David C. Rapoport, "Coup d'État: The View of the Men Firing Pistols," in Friedrich, ed., *Revolution*, pp. 53–74. *Cf.* Edward Luttwak, *Coup d'État: A Practical Handbook* (New York: Fawcett Books, 1969), p. 12.

10. See Charles Tilly, *The Vendée* (Cambridge, Mass.: Harvard University Press, 1964), pp. 1–6 *et passim.*

CHAPTER 3

1. Harry Eckstein, "On the Etiology of Internal War," *History and Theory*, 4 (1965); reprinted in Eric A. Nordlinger, ed., *Politics and Society: Studies in Comparative Political Sociology* (Englewood Cliffs, N.J.: Prentice-Hall, Inc., 1970), pp. 291 ff. A corresponding distinction between "dysfunctions" and "accelerators" is made in Chalmers Johnson, *Revolution and the Social System* (Stanford University: Hoover Institution on War, Revolution, and Peace, 1964); Johnson, *Revolutionary Change* (Boston: Little, Brown & Co., 1966).

2. For a provocative general treatment of this subject, see Eckstein, "On the Etiology of Internal War." See also Aristotle, *The Politics of Aristotle*, translated with an Introduction and Notes by Ernest Barker (New York: Oxford University Press, 1958), Book V; Crane Brinton, *The Anatomy of Revolution* (New York: Vintage Books, 1956); James C. Davies, "Toward a Theory of Revolution," *American Sociological Review*, 27 (February 1962), pp. 5–19; Alexis de Tocqueville, *The Old Regime and the French Revolution* (1856) (New York: Anchor Books, 1955); Lyford P. Edwards, *The Natural History of Revolution* (Chicago: University of Chicago Press, 1927); Ivo K. and Rosalind L. Feierabend, "Aggressive Behaviors Within Polities, 1948–1962: A Cross-National Study," *Journal of Conflict Resolution*, 10 (1966), pp. 249–71; James A. Geschwender, "Explorations in the Theory of Social Movements and Revolts," *Social Forces*, 47 (December 1968), pp. 127–36; Ted Robert Gurr, *Why Men Rebel* (Princeton, N.J.: Princeton University Press, 1970); Johnson, *Revolution and the Social System*; Johnson, *Revolutionary Change*; Carl Leiden and Karl M. Schmitt, *The Politics of Violence: Revolution in the Modern World* (Englewood Cliffs, N.J.: Prentice-Hall,

Inc., 1968); George S. Pettee, *The Process of Revolution* (New York: Harper & Bros., 1938); Bruce M. Russett, "Inequality and Instability: The Relation of Land Tenure to Politics," *World Politics*, 16 (April 1964), pp. 442–54; David C. Schwartz, "A Theory of Revolutionary Behavior," in James C. Davies, ed., *When Men Revolt—And Why* (New York: Free Press, 1971); Raymond Tanter and Manus Midlarsky, "A Theory of Revolution," *Journal of Conflict Resolution*, 11 (1967), pp. 264–80; David Willer and George K. Zollschan, "Prolegomena to a Theory of Revolutions," in Zollschan and Walter Hirsch, eds., *Explorations in Social Change* (Boston: Houghton Mifflin Co., 1964).

3. Eckstein, "On the Etiology of Internal War," pp. 291–93; Johnson, *Revolution and the Social System*, p. 12; Johnson, *Revolutionary Change*, pp. 99 ff.

4. For a useful summary of the evolution of the concept of strategy, see Bernard Brodie, "Strategy," *International Encyclopedia of the Social Sciences*, Vol. 15 (New York: Macmillan Co. and Free Press, 1968).

5. Quoted in B. H. Liddell Hart, *Strategy* (New York: Frederick A. Praeger, revised edition, 1954), p. 333.

6. Ibid., pp. 335–36.

7. Beaufre, *An Introduction to Strategy* (New York: Frederick A. Praeger, 1965), p. 22 (italics in original).

8. Wylie, *Military Strategy: A General Theory of Power Control* (New Brunswick, N.J.: Rutgers University Press, 1967), pp. 110, 111, 91.

9. Hoffer, *The True Believer: Thoughts on the Nature of Mass Movements* (New York: New American Library, 1958), pp. 119 ff.

10. Ibid., p. 131.

11. There is a striking resemblance between the qualities of the leaders specified by Hoffer and those specified by Gaetano Mosca. See Mosca, *The Ruling Class* (New York: McGraw-Hill Book Co., 1939); Mosca, "The Final Version of the Theory of the Ruling Class," in James H. Meisel, *The Myth of the Ruling Class* (Ann Arbor, Mich.: University of Michigan Press, 1958). In a less elaborate fashion Robert C. Tucker has identified three major attributes of the "radical mind": (1) a total repudiation of the existing society, (2) a utopian vision of an alternative, perfect social order, and (3) an activism that propels the individual toward a revolutionary transformation of society and "the world as it ought to be." Tucker, "The Deradicalization of Marxist Movements," *American Political Science Review*, 61 (June 1967), pp. 343–58.

12. Hopper, "The Revolutionary Process: A Frame of Reference for the Study of Revolutionary Movements," *Social Forces*, 28 (1950), pp. 270–79.

13. A less elaborate classification has been put forth by Robert C. North and Ithiel de Sola Pool, who distinguish three types of revolutionary leaders: the manipulators of symbols, the managers of violence, and the organizers. North and Pool, "Kuomintang and

Chinese Communist Elites," in Harold D. Lasswell and Daniel Lerner, eds., *World Revolutionary Elites* (Cambridge, Mass.: M.I.T. Press, 1965), pp. 386–87. In his study of the Asian Communist leaders, Robert A. Scalapino identifies three types: the ideologue, the activist, and the careerist. "Communism in Asia: Toward a Comparative Analysis," in Scalapino, ed., *The Communist Revolution in Asia* (Englewood Cliffs, N.J.: Prentice-Hall, Inc., 1965), pp. 7 ff.

14. Brinton, *The Anatomy of Revolution*, p. 110.

15. Schueller, "The Politburo," in Lasswell and Lerner, eds., *World Revolutionary Elites*, p. 111.

16. North and Pool, "Kuomintang and Chinese Communist Elites," p. 383.

17. Lee, "The Founders of the Chinese Communist Party: A Study in Revolutionaries," *Civilizations*, 13 (1968), p. 115.

18. Scalapino, "Communism in Asia," p. 15.

19. Brinton, *The Anatomy of Revolution*, p. 107.

20. Schueller, "The Politburo," pp. 103–4, 119–21.

21. Lee, "The Founders of the Chinese Communist Party," pp. 117–18, 120.

22. Scalapino, "Communism in Asia," p. 14.

23. Kautsky, "Revolutionary and Managerial Elites in Modernizing Regimes," *Comparative Politics*, 1 (July 1969), p. 446.

24. Brinton, *The Anatomy of Revolution*, p. 107.

25. Scalapino, "Communism in Asia," p. 14.

26. Kautsky, "Revolutionary and Managerial Elites in Modernizing Regimes," p. 445.

27. Lee, "The Founders of the Chinese Communist Party," pp. 115, 119.

28. For a more elaborate treatment of the concept of ideology, see M. Rejai, "Political Ideology: Theoretical and Comparative Perspectives," in Rejai, ed., *Decline of Ideology?* (New York: Aldine-Atherton, 1971) and the sources cited therein.

29. Giovanni Sartori, "Politics, Ideology, and Belief Systems," *American Political Science Review*, 63 (June 1969), p. 411.

30. Selznick, *The Organizational Weapon: A Study of Bolshevik Strategy and Tactics* (New York: McGraw-Hill Book Co., 1952), p. 10. *Cf.* Samuel H. Barnes, "Ideology and the Organization of Conflict: On the Relationship Between Political Thought and Behavior," *Journal of Politics*, 28 (August 1966), pp. 521 ff.

31. Selznick, *The Organizational Weapon*, p. 8.

32. Huntington, *Political Order in Changing Societies* (New Haven, Conn.: Yale University Press, 1968), p. 461.

33. Lenin, *What Is to Be Done?* (1902) (New York: International Publishers, 1929), pp. 114 ff.

34. See Snow, *Red Star Over China* (1938) (New York: Grove Press, reprinted 1961), p. 94.

35. Guevara, *Guerrilla Warfare* (New York: Vintage Books, 1961), p. 112.

36. Quoted in Theodore Draper, *Castroism: Theory and Practice* (New York: Frederick A. Praeger, 1965), p. 41.

37. E. V. Walter, *Terror and Resistance: A Study of Political Violence* (New York: Oxford University Press, 1969), p. 7.

38. For a wide-ranging discussion of "regimes of terror" or "rule by terror," see ibid. Walter explicitly excludes "revolutionary governments" from his treatment, however (p. viii).

39. For a more elaborate discussion of this topic see Thomas Perry Thornton, "Terror as a Weapon of Agitation," in Harry Eckstein, ed., *Internal War: Problems and Approaches* (New York: Free Press, 1964).

40. For an excellent treatment of this topic, on which the present discussion heavily relies, see James N. Rosenau, ed., *International Aspects of Civil Strife* (Princeton, N.J.: Princeton University Press, 1964), in particular George Modelski's "The International Relations of Internal War." See also George A. Kelly and Linda B. Miller, *Internal War and International Systems: Perspectives on Method* (Harvard University: Center for International Affairs, 1969); Sigmund Neumann, "The International Civil War," *World Politics*, 1 (1949), pp. 333–50.

41. For an earlier, partial application of the scheme, see M. Rejai, "Guerrilla Communism: China, North Vietnam, Cuba," in Reo M. Christenson et al., *Ideologies and Modern Politics* (New York: Dodd, Mead & Co., 1971).

CHAPTER 4

1. Quoted in Dwight B. Heath, "Bolivia: Peasant Syndicates Among the Aymara of the Yungas—A View from the Grass Roots," in Henry A. Landsberger, ed., *Latin American Peasant Movements* (Ithaca, N.Y.: Cornell University Press, 1969), pp. 178–79.

2. Alberto Ostria Gutiérrez, *The Tragedy of Bolivia: A People Crucified* (New York: Devin-Adair Co., 1958), pp. 159–60.

3. Robert J. Alexander, *The Bolivian National Revolution* (New Brunswick, N.J.: Rutgers University Press, 1958), p. 16. The description is Víctor Paz Estenssoro's.

4. Heath, "Bolivia: Peasant Syndicates Among the Aymara of the Yungas—A View from the Grass Roots," pp. 178, 183; Dwight B. Heath et al., *Land Reform and Social Revolution in Bolivia* (New York: Frederick A. Praeger, 1969), p. 383.

5. Foreign Areas Studies Division, Special Operations Research Office, The American University, *U. S. Army Area Handbook for Bolivia* (Washington, D.C.: Government Printing Office, 1963), p. 463.

6. Hubert Herring, *A History of Latin America* (New York: Alfred A. Knopf, 1962), p. 558.

7. Charles H. Weston, "An Ideology of Modernization: The Case

of the Bolivian MNR," *Journal of Inter-American Studies,* 10 (January 1968), p. 87.

8. Between 1938 and 1952 alone, the cost of living rose by nearly 1200 per cent. For exact figures on a year-by-year basis, see Herbert S. Klein, *Parties and Political Change in Bolivia, 1880–1952* (Cambridge, Eng.: Cambridge University Press, 1969), p. 387.

9. Weston, "An Ideology of Modernization: The Case of the Bolivian MNR," p. 90.

10. See especially Klein, *Parties and Political Change in Bolivia, passim;* Ostria, *The Tragedy of Bolivia, passim;* William S. Stokes, "The 'Revolución Nacional' and the MNR in Bolivia," *Inter-American Economic Affairs,* 12 (Spring 1959), pp. 28–53; Weston, "An Ideology of Modernization: The Case of the Bolivian MNR," pp. 85–101.

11. Quoted in Alexander, *The Bolivian National Revolution,* p. 59.

12. Herring, *A History of Latin America,* pp. 561–62. *Cf. U. S. Army Area Handbook for Bolivia,* p. 406.

13. Alexander, *The Bolivian National Revolution,* pp. 95–96.

14. Weston, "An Ideology of Modernization: The Case of the Bolivian MNR," p. 94.

15. Quoted in Alexander, *The Bolivian National Revolution,* p. 31.

16. Richard W. Patch, "Personalities and Politics in Bolivia," *AUFS Reports: West Coast South America Series,* Vol. IX (New York: American Universities Field Staff, Inc., 1962), p. 4. For a more detailed discussion of this topic see Klein, *Parties and Political Change in Bolivia,* pp. 337, 372, 396 *et passim.*

17. Herring, *A History of Latin America,* p. 561, n. 7. The same point is made in Arthur P. Whitaker, *The United States and South America: The Northern Republics* (Cambridge, Mass.: Harvard University Press, 1948), p. 120; James M. Malloy, *Bolivia: The Uncompleted Revolution* (Pittsburgh, Pa.: University of Pittsburgh Press, 1970), p. 117.

18. See Luis Peñaloza, *Historia del Movimiento Nacionalista Revolucionario, 1941–1952* (La Paz: Editorial Librería "Juventud," 1963), esp. Chapter 14. *Cf. U. S. Army Area Handbook for Bolivia,* esp. p. 351; Malloy, *Bolivia,* p. 137.

19. Alexander, *The Bolivian National Revolution,* p. 41.

20. Richard W. Patch, "Bolivia: U.S. Assistance in a Revolutionary Setting," in Richard Adams et al., *Social Change in Latin America Today* (New York: Harper & Bros., 1963), p. 118.

21. Peñaloza, *Historia del Movimiento Nacionalista Revolucionario,* pp. 256 ff., 271; Malloy, *Bolivia,* pp. 137–38.

22. Herbert S. Klein, "The Crisis of Legitimacy and the Origins of Social Revolution: The Bolivian Experience," *Journal of Inter-American Studies,* 10 (January 1968), p. 113.

23. Ostria, *The Tragedy of Bolivia, passim.*

24. Alexander, *The Bolivian National Revolution,* p. 37.

25. Ostria, *The Tragedy of Bolivia,* p. 81.

26. Alexander, *The Bolivian National Revolution,* p. 273.

27. Patch, "Personalities and Politics in Bolivia," p. 4.

28. See Whitaker, *The United States and South America*, p. 140; Ostria, *The Tragedy of Bolivia*, pp. 15–17.

29. Ostria, *The Tragedy of Bolivia*, p. 35.

30. Patch, "Bolivia: U.S. Assistance in a Revolutionary Setting," pp. 151 ff.; Weston, "An Ideology of Modernization: The Case of the Bolivian MNR," p. 86.

31. Quoted in Ostria, *The Tragedy of Bolivia*, pp. 18–19.

32. Quoted in Alexander, *The Bolivian National Revolution*, pp. 32–33.

33. Ostria, *The Tragedy of Bolivia*, p. 177.

CHAPTER 5

1. See Joseph Buttinger, *Vietnam: A Political History* (New York: Frederick A. Praeger, 1968), p. 123.

2. John T. McAlister, Jr., *Viet Nam: The Origins of Revolution* (New York: Alfred A. Knopf, 1969), esp. pp. 325 ff.

3. Precise figures are in Douglas Pike, *Viet Cong* (Cambridge, Mass.: M.I.T. Press, 1966), p. 41.

4. The data on the Vietminh leaders have been compiled from the following sources: Richard Critchfield, *The Long Charade: Political Subversion in the Vietnam War* (New York: Harcourt, Brace & World, 1968), pp. 44 ff.; Bernard B. Fall, "Ho Chi Minh: A Profile," in Fall, ed., *Ho Chi Minh on Revolution* (New York: Signet Books, 1968); Fall, "Vo Nguyên Giap—Man and Myth," in Giap, *People's War, People's Army* (New York: Bantam Books, 1968); Fall, *The Two Vietnams: A Political and Military Analysis*, 2nd ed. (New York: Frederick A. Praeger, 1967); Hoang Van Chi, *From Colonialism to Communism: A Case History of North Vietnam* (New York: Frederick A. Praeger, 1964), pp. 36 ff.; J. P. Honey, *Communism in North Vietnam* (Cambridge, Mass.: M.I.T. Press, 1963), pp. 24 ff.; Jean Lacouture, "Uncle Ho's 'Best Nephew' is Pham Van Dong . . . ," *The New York Times Magazine*, May 19, 1968, pp. 26 ff.; McAlister, *Viet Nam: The Origins of Revolution*, pp. 142 ff., 152 ff.; Edgar O'Ballance, *The Indo-China War, 1945–54* (London: Faber & Faber, 1964), pp. 30 ff.

5. McAlister, *Viet Nam: The Origins of Revolution*, p. 153; O'Ballance, *The Indo-China War*, p. 43.

6. Buttinger, *Vietnam: A Political History*, p. 332.

7. See, for example, M. Rejai, ed., *Mao Tse-tung on Revolution and War* (Garden City, N.Y.: Doubleday & Co., 1969), Chapter IV.

8. The Three Rules are: "(1) Obey orders in all your actions. (2) Don't take a single needle or piece of thread from the masses. (3) Turn in everything captured." The Eight Points read: "(1) Speak politely. (2) Pay fairly for what you buy. (3) Return everything you borrow. (4) Pay for anything you damage. (5) Don't hit or swear at people. (6) Don't damage crops. (7) Don't take liberties

with women. (8) Don't ill-treat captives." Mao Tse-tung, "On the Reissue of the Three Main Rules of Discipline and the Eight Points for Attention—Instruction of the General Headquarters of the Chinese People's Liberation Army" (October 1947), *Selected Works of Mao Tse-tung,* IV (Peking: Foreign Languages Press, 1961), p. 155.

9. Text in Fall, ed., *Ho Chi Minh on Revolution,* pp. 141–43.

10. Among the best sources on this topic are Buttinger, *Vietnam: A Political History;* Fall, *Street Without Joy* (Harrisburg, Pa.: Stackpole, 1963); Fall, *The Two Vietnams;* McAlister, *Viet Nam: The Origins of Revolution.*

11. A detailed comparison of Mao and Giap is in Michael Elliott-Bateman, *Defeat in the East: The Mark of Mao Tse-tung on War* (London: Oxford University Press, 1967).

12. Among the best sources on Vietminh military organization are O'Ballance, *The Indo-China War;* and George K. Tanham, *Communist Revolutionary Warfare: From the Vietminh to the Viet Cong,* revised ed. (New York: Frederick A. Praeger, 1967).

13. "A Single Spark Can Start a Prairie Fire" (January 1930), *Selected Works of Mao Tse-tung,* I (Peking: Foreign Languages Press, 1964), p. 124.

14. O'Ballance, *The Indo-China War,* p. 198.

15. Particularly good accounts of Dien Bien Phu include Fall, *Hell in a Very Small Place: The Siege of Dien Bien Phu* (New York: Vintage Books, 1968); Fall, *Street Without Joy;* Giap, *People's War, People's Army;* and O'Ballance, *The Indo-China War.*

16. Buttinger, *Vietnam: A Political History,* p. 180 *et passim.*

17. Fall, *Street Without Joy,* p. 30.

18. O'Ballance, *The Indo-China War,* p. 198.

19. Ibid., p. 199.

CHAPTER 6

1. Daniel and Gabriel Cohn-Bendit, *Obsolete Communism: The Left-Wing Alternative* (New York: McGraw-Hill Book Co., 1968), p. 57.

2. Aron, *The Elusive Revolution: Anatomy of a Student Revolt* (New York: Frederick A. Praeger, 1969), p. 1.

3. Quoted in Cohn-Bendit, *Obsolete Communism,* p. 59.

4. For an account of police attitudes toward the events of May, see Paul Gillet, "Inside the Prefecture," in Charles Posner, ed., *Reflections on the Revolution in France: 1968* (London: Penguin Books, 1970), pp. 163–71.

5. Aron, *The Elusive Revolution,* p. ix.

6. On the extent of popular involvement, see, in particular, Posner, ed., *Reflections on the Revolution in France;* Allan Priaulx and Sanford J. Unger, *The Almost Revolution, France—1968* (New York: Dell Publishing Co., 1969); Patrick Seale and Maureen Mc-

Conville, *Red Flag/Black Flag: French Revolution, 1968* (New York: Ballantine Books, 1968).

7. See, for example, Cohn-Bendit, *Obsolete Communism*, pp. 68, 70–71.

8. Seale and McConville, *Red Flag/Black Flag*, p. 213.

9. See, for example, Charles Posner, "Chronology," in Posner, ed., *Reflections on the Revolution in France*, p. 104.

10. Brinton, *The Anatomy of Revolution* (New York: Vintage Books, 1952), p. 31.

11. Posner, "Chronology," in Posner, ed., *Reflections on the Revolution in France*, p. 58.

12. For a sampling of student slogans, which will be used frequently in the course of this chapter, see, for example, Posner, ed., *Reflections on the Revolution in France*, *passim;* Priaulx and Unger, *The Almost Revolution*, pp. 152–53 *et passim;* Angelo Quattrocchi and Tom Nairn, *The Beginning of the End: France, May 1968* (London: Panther Books, Ltd., 1968), pp. 50–52 *et passim;* Seale and McConville, *Red Flag/Black Flag*, *passim.*

13. Bernard E. Brown, *The French Revolt: May 1968* (New York: McCaleb-Seiler Publishing Co., 1970), p. 15.

14. Alain Geismar, transcript of interview in Hervé Bourges, ed., *The French Student Revolt: The Leaders Speak* (New York: Hill & Wang, 1968), p. 29.

15. Aron, *The Elusive Revolution*, p. 44; *cf.* Geismar, transcript of interview in Bourges, ed., *The French Student Revolt*, p. 33.

16. Cohn-Bendit, *Obsolete Communism*, pp. 251, 58, 249–50.

17. "Daniel Cohn-Bendit Interviewed by Jean-Paul Sartre," in Bourges, ed., *The French Student Revolt*, pp. 77–78.

18. Geismar, transcript of interview in Bourges, ed., *The French Student Revolt*, p. 37.

19. Sauvageot, transcript of interview in Bourges, ed., *The French Student Revolt*, pp. 15, 20.

20. Bourges, *The French Student Revolt*, p. 4.

21. Ibid., p. 5.

22. Seale and McConville, *Red Flag/Black Flag*, p. 49.

23. "Daniel Cohn-Bendit Interviewed by Jean-Paul Sartre," in Bourges, ed., *The French Student Revolt*, p. 79.

24. Geismar, transcript of interview in Bourges, ed., *The French Student Revolt*, pp. 36–37.

25. Cohn-Bendit, transcript of interview in Bourges, ed., *The French Student Revolt*, p. 58; *cf.* Cohn-Bendit, *Obsolete Communism*, p. 58.

26. Cohn-Bendit, *Obsolete Communism*, p. 35 *et passim;* Sauvageot, transcript of interview in Bourges, ed., *The French Student Revolt*, pp. 11–12; André Gorz, "What Are the Lessons of the May Events?" in Posner, ed., *Reflections on the Revolution in France*, p. 258.

27. Cohn-Bendit, *Obsolete Communism*, p. 27.

28. Sauvageot, transcript of interview in Bourges, ed., *The French Student Revolt*, p. 25.

29. Cohn-Bendit, *Obsolete Communism*, pp. 35 ff., 51; *cf.* René Lourau, "Sociology and Politics in 1968," in Posner, ed., *Reflections on the Revolution in France*, pp. 225–38.

30. Gorz, "What Are the Lessons of the May Events?" in Posner, ed., *Reflections on the Revolution in France*, p. 255.

31. Cohn-Bendit, *Obsolete Communism*, p. 48.

32. Ibid., p. 255.

33. Vigier, "The Action Committees," in Posner, ed., *Reflections on the Revolution in France*, pp. 203–4.

34. Cohn-Bendit, transcript of interview in Bourges, ed., *The French Student Revolt*, p. 52.

35. For detailed treatment of the attitude of the revolutionaries toward the PCF and the other parties of the left, as well as the traditional left's attitude toward the May revolution, see, for example, Bourges, ed., *The French Student Revolt, passim;* Cohn-Bendit, *Obsolete Communism, passim;* George Lichtheim, "What Happened in France," *Commentary,* 46 (September 1968), pp. 39–49; Arthur P. Mendel, "Why the French Communists Stopped the Revolution," *Review of Politics,* 31 (January 1969), pp. 3–27; Posner, ed., *Reflections on the Revolution in France, passim;* Seale and McConville, *Red Flag/Black Flag*, esp. pp. 154 ff.; Edmond Taylor, "Revolution and Reaction in France," *Foreign Affairs,* 47 (October 1968), pp. 99–109; Frank L. Wilson, "The French Left and the Elections of 1968," *World Politics,* 21 (July 1969), pp. 539–74.

36. Geismar, transcript of interview in Bourges, ed., *The French Student Revolt*, p. 39.

37. Ibid., p. 42.

38. Stanley Hoffman, "The French Psychodrama: de Gaulle's Anti-Communist Coup," *The New Republic,* 159 (August 31, 1968), p. 16.

39. Geismar, "Round Table on Radio Luxembourg (extracts)," in Bourges, ed., *The French Student Revolt*, p. 69.

40. Cohn-Bendit, *Obsolete Communism*, p. 105.

41. Ibid., pp. 105 ff.; Cohn-Bendit, transcript of interview in Bourges, ed., *The French Student Revolt*, p. 55.

42. Cohn-Bendit, *Obsolete Communism*, p. 112.

43. See note 12 above.

44. Hoffman, "The French Psychodrama," p. 16.

45. Seale and McConville, *Red Flag/Black Flag*, pp. 88–89.

46. Posner, "Introduction," in Posner, ed., *Reflections on the Revolution in France*, p. 43.

47. Cohn-Bendit, *Obsolete Communism*, pp. 63–64.

48. "Daniel Cohn-Bendit Interviewed by Jean-Paul Sartre," in Bourges, ed., *The French Student Revolt*, p. 79.

49. See Aron, *The Elusive Revolution*, pp. xv, 4, 20, 25–26, *et passim*.

50. See esp. André Glucksmann, "Action," in Posner, ed., *Re-*

flections on the Revolution in France, pp. 185–98; Henri Lefebvre, *The Explosion: Marxism and the French Revolution* (New York: Monthly Review Press, 1969), Chapter 7.

51. Cohn-Bendit, transcript of interview in Bourges, ed., *The French Student Revolt*, p. 52.

52. Vigier, "The Action Committees," p. 208 *et passim*.

53. Geismar, transcript of interview in Bourges, ed., *The French Student Revolt*, pp. 46–47; *cf.* Glucksmann, "Action," in Posner, ed., *Reflections on the Revolution in France*, p. 195.

54. Cohn-Bendit, *Obsolete Communism*, pp. 13–14; "Daniel Cohn-Bendit Interviewed by Jean-Paul Sartre," in Bourges, ed., *The French Student Revolt*, p. 83.

55. Sauvageot, transcript of interview in Bourges, ed., *The French Student Revolt*, p. 23.

56. Cohn-Bendit, transcript of interview in Bourges, ed., *The French Student Revolt*, p. 60.

57. "Daniel Cohn-Bendit Interviewed by Jean-Paul Sartre," in Bourges, ed., *The French Student Revolt*, p. 79; Cohn-Bendit, transcript of interview in Bourges, ed., *The French Student Revolt*, p. 58; Cohn-Bendit, *Obsolete Communism*, pp. 199, 255–56, 249.

58. Cohn-Bendit, *Obsolete Communism*, p. 79.

59. Ibid., p. 199.

60. Sauvageot, transcript of interview in Bourges, ed., *The French Student Revolt*, p. 22.

61. Ibid., p. 15.

62. Seale and McConville, *Red Flag/Black Flag*, p. 62.

63. "Serve the People" is a famous slogan of Mao Tse-tung's and the title of a well-known Mao article. See *Selected Works of Mao Tse-tung*, III (Peking: Foreign Languages Press, 1965), pp. 227–28.

64. Quoted in Seale and McConville, *Red Flag/Black Flag*, p. 61.

65. Cohn-Bendit, *Obsolete Communism*, pp. 80 ff.

66. Vigier, "Action Committees," in Posner, ed., *Reflections on the Revolution in France*, p. 199.

67. Cohn-Bendit, *Obsolete Communism*, p. 92 *et passim*.

68. Barjonet, "CGT 1968: Subjectivism to the Rescue of the Status Quo," in Posner, ed., *Reflections on the Revolution in France*, esp. pp. 160, 162.

69. For detailed treatment of the activities of the CGT and the PCF, as well as other trade unions and parties of the left, see sources cited in note 35 above.

70. Cohn-Bendit, *Obsolete Communism*, p. 64.

71. Ibid., p. 120.

72. Gillet, "Inside the Prefecture" (note 4 above), p. 167.

73. See, for example, Priaulx and Unger, *The Almost Revolution*, pp. 38–40, 45, 101, 109–10, 141–42.

74. *The Washington Post*, July 19, 1970.

75. Cohn-Bendit, *Obsolete Communism*, p. 17.

76. Sauvageot, transcript of interview in Bourges, ed., *The French Student Revolt*, p. 14.

77. Ibid., p. 28.

78. *Peking Review,* May 24, 1968, p. 19. See also the issues of May 31, June 14, June 21, and July 12, 1968.

79. Cohn-Bendit, transcript of interview in Bourges, *The French Student Revolt,* p. 57.

CHAPTER 7

1. Daniel and Gabriel Cohn-Bendit, *Obsolete Communism: The Left-Wing Alternative* (New York: McGraw-Hill Book Co., 1968), p. 154.

2. Ibid., p. 71.

3. Debray's main work is *Revolution in the Revolution? Armed Struggle and Political Struggle in Latin America* (New York: Grove Press, 1967). For a convenient summary of Castro's view, see Theodore Draper, *Castroism: Theory and Practice* (New York: Frederick A. Praeger, 1965). For Guevara, see his *Guerrilla Warfare* (New York: Vintage Books, 1961). For a more elaborate general treatment of this theme, see M. Rejai, "Guerrilla Communism: China, North Vietnam, Cuba," in Reo M. Christenson et al., *Ideologies and Modern Politics* (New York: Dodd, Mead & Co., 1971).

4. "Problems of War and Strategy" (November 1938), *Selected Works of Mao Tse-tung,* II (Peking: Foreign Languages Press, 1965), p. 224.

5. Debray, *Revolution in the Revolution?,* p. 106 (italics in original).

6. The Chinese response to the Cuban challenge to Mao's doctrines was quite predictable. An unsigned article in the official weekly *Peking Review* approvingly discussed a statement by the Communist Party of France denouncing the "fallacies of Régis Debray." The Chinese portrayed Debray's book as "a big counterrevolutionary mystification and . . . in essence an attack on Marxism-Leninism, Mao Tse-tung's thought." They dismissed Debray's "purely military viewpoint" and his "preposterous" attack upon the "correct theses of Chairman Mao Tse-tung." See "Marxism-Leninism, Mao Tse-tung's Thought, Is Universal Truth," *Peking Review,* July 26, 1968, pp. 11–12.

7. Leites and Wolf, *Rebellion and Authority: An Analytic Essay on Insurgent Conflicts* (Chicago: Markham Publishing Co., 1970), p. 149 (italics in original).

8. Thornton, "Terror as a Weapon of Political Agitation," in Harry Eckstein, ed., *Internal War: Problems and Approaches* (New York: Free Press, 1964), p. 90.

9. Guevara's approach, with its emphasis on subverting imperialism from the inside, stands in sharp contrast to (while at the same time complementing) the traditional Communist advocacy of an international strategy toward the imperialist countries. One of the most striking illustrations of the latter is found in Lin Piao,

Mao Tse-tung's former heir apparent. In an attempt to project on the global level the revolutionary strategy of Mao, Lin insists that "Mao Tse-tung's theory of the establishment of rural revolutionary base areas and the encirclement of the cities from the countryside is of outstanding and universal practical importance for the present revolutionary struggles of all the oppressed nations and peoples." He adds emphatically, "Taking the entire globe, if North America and Western Europe can be called 'the cities of the world,' then Asia, Africa, and Latin America constitute 'the rural areas of the world.' . . . In a sense, the contemporary world revolution also presents a picture of the encirclement of cities by the rural areas. In the final analysis, the whole cause of world revolution hinges on the revolutionary struggles of the Asian, African, and Latin American peoples, who make up the overwhelming majority of the world's population. The socialist countries should regard it as their internationalist duty to support the people's revolutionary struggles in Asia, Africa, and Latin America." Lin Piao, *Long Live the Victory of People's War!* (Peking: Foreign Languages Press, 1965), pp. 47, 48–49.

10. Cohn-Bendit, *Obsolete Communism*, pp. 17, 252. *Cf.* Staughton Lynd, "Almost Making It: One View on the Meaning of France's Revolution," *Commonweal*, June 6, 1969, pp. 345–47.

11. See especially Hugh Davis Graham and Ted Robert Gurr, eds., *Violence in America: Historical and Comparative Perspectives* (New York: Signet Books, 1969); Jerome H. Skolnick, *The Politics of Protest* (New York: Ballantine Books, 1969). See also Lynne B. Iglitzin, *Violent Conflict in American Society* (San Francisco: Chandler Publishing Co., 1972); Richard E. Rubenstein, *Rebels in Eden: Mass Political Violence in the United States* (Boston: Little, Brown & Co., 1970).

12. Gurr, "A Comparative Study of Civil Strife," in Graham and Gurr, eds., *Violence in America*, pp. 544–605.

13. Richard Maxwell Brown, "Historical Patterns of Violence in America," in Graham and Gurr, eds., *Violence in America*, p. 70.

14. Graham and Gurr, "Introduction," in Graham and Gurr, eds., *Violence in America*, p. xiii.

15. Joe B. Frantz, "The Frontier Tradition: An Invitation to Violence," in Graham and Gurr, eds., *Violence in America*, pp. 119–43.

16. See, for example, Philip Taft and Philip Ross, "American Labor Violence: Its Causes, Character, and Outcome," in Graham and Gurr, eds., *Violence in America*, pp. 270–376.

17. For a comprehensive examination of the relationship between mass media and violence, see Robert K. Baker and Sandra J. Ball, *Violence and the Media* (Washington, D.C.: U. S. Government Printing Office, 1969).

18. Shoup, "The New American Militarism," *The Atlantic*, April 1969, p. 53.

19. See, for example, Raymond Aron, *The Elusive Revolution: Anatomy of a Student Revolt* (New York: Frederick A. Praeger,

1969), *passim;* John Ardagh, *The New French Revolution* (New York: Harper & Row, 1969), esp. pp. 462–63.

20. See Marcuse, *One Dimensional Man* (Boston: Beacon Press, 1964); Marcuse, *An Essay on Liberation* (Boston: Beacon Press, 1969).

21. Jean-Pierre Vigier, "The Action Committees," in Charles Posner, ed., *Reflections on the Revolution in France: 1968* (Baltimore: Penguin Books, 1970), pp. 206, 210–11.

22. For a comprehensive discussion of urban guerrilla activity and some of its potential consequences, see Martin Oppenheimer, *The Urban Guerrilla* (Chicago: Quadrangle Books, 1969). See also Barrington Moore, Jr., "Revolution in America?" *The New York Review of Books,* January 30, 1969, pp. 6 ff.

23. *Cf.* Frank Tannenbaum, "On Political Stability," *Political Science Quarterly,* 76 (1960), pp. 161–80.

BIBLIOGRAPHY

GENERAL THEORETICAL WORKS

Adams, Brooks. *The Theory of Social Revolutions.* New York: Macmillan Co., 1913.

Amann, Peter H. "Revolution: A Redefinition." *Political Science Quarterly,* 77 (1962), pp. 36–53.

Arendt, Hannah. *On Revolution.* New York: Viking Press, 1963.

———. *On Violence.* New York: Harcourt, Brace & World, 1969.

———. "Reflections on Violence." *Journal of International Affairs,* 23 (1969), pp. 1–35.

Aristotle. *The Politics of Aristotle,* translated with an Introduction and Notes by Ernest Barker. New York: Oxford University Press, 1958, Book V.

Baker, Robert K. and Sandra J. Ball. *Violence and the Media,* A Staff Report of the National Commission on the Causes and Prevention of Violence, Vol. 9. Washington, D.C.: U. S. Government Printing Office, 1969.

Barnes, Samuel H. "Ideology and the Organization of Conflict: On the Relationship Between Political Thought and Behavior." *Journal of Politics,* 28 (August 1966), pp. 513–30.

Beaufre, André. *An Introduction to Strategy.* New York: Frederick A. Praeger, 1965.

Bienen, Henry. *Violence and Social Change: A Review of Current Literature.* Chicago: The University of Chicago Press, 1968.

Black, Cyril E., ed. *Communism and Revolution: The Strategic Uses of Political Violence.* Princeton, N.J.: Princeton University Press, 1964.

Brinton, Crane. *The Anatomy of Revolution.* New York: Vintage Books, 1956.

Brodie, Bernard. "Strategy." *International Encyclopedia of the Social Sciences.* New York: Macmillan Co. and Free Press, 1968.

Calvert, Peter. *Revolution.* New York: Praeger Publishers, 1970.

——. "Revolution: The Politics of Violence." *Political Studies,* 15 (1967), pp. 1–11.

Coser, Lewis A. *The Functions of Social Conflict.* New York: Free Press, 1956.

——. "Some Social Functions of Violence." *The Annals,* 364 (March 1966), pp. 8–18.

Davies, James C. "The Circumstances and Causes of Revolution: A Review." *Journal of Conflict Resolution,* 11 (1967), pp. 247–57.

——. "Toward a Theory of Revolution." *American Sociological Review,* 27 (February 1962), pp. 5–19.

——, ed. *When Men Revolt—And Why.* New York: Free Press, 1971.

Debray, Régis. *Revolution in the Revolution? Armed Struggle and Political Struggle in Latin America.* New York: Grove Press, 1967.

Eckstein, Harry. "On the Etiology of Internal War." *History and Theory,* 4 (1965), pp. 133–63. Reprinted in Eric A. Nordlinger, ed. *Politics and Society: Studies in Comparative Political Sociology.* Englewood Cliffs, N.J.: Prentice-Hall, Inc., 1970.

——, ed. *Internal War: Problems and Approaches.* New York: Free Press, 1964.

Edwards, Lyford P. *The Natural History of Revolution.* Chicago: University of Chicago Press, 1927.

Ellwood, Charles A. "A Psychological Theory of Revolutions." *American Journal of Sociology,* 11 (1905–6), pp. 49–59.

Fanon, Frantz. *The Wretched of the Earth.* New York: Grove Press, 1968.

Feierabend, Ivo K. and Rosalind L. Feierabend. "Aggressive Behaviors Within Polities, 1948–1962: A Cross-National Study." *Journal of Conflict Resolution,* 10 (1966), pp. 249–71.

Flanigan, William H. and Edwin Fogelman. "Patterns of Political Violence in Comparative Historical Perspective." *Comparative Politics,* 3 (October 1970), pp. 1–20.

Friedrich, Carl J., ed. *Revolution.* New York: Atherton Press, 1967.

Geschwender, James A. "Explorations in the Theory of Social Movements and Revolts." *Social Forces,* 47 (December 1968), pp. 127–36.

Gillis, John R. "Political Decay and the European Revolutions, 1789–1848." *World Politics,* 22 (April 1970), pp. 344–70.

Goodspeed, D. J. *The Conspirators: A Study of the Coup d'Etat.* London: Macmillan & Co., 1962.

Gottschalk, Louis. "Causes of Revolution." *American Journal of Sociology,* 50 (1944), pp. 1–8.

Graham, Hugh Davis and Ted Robert Gurr, eds. *Violence in America: Historical and Comparative Perspectives.* New York: Signet Books, 1969.

Gross, Feliks. *The Seizure of Political Power in a Century of Revolutions.* New York: Philosophical Library, 1958.

Groth, Alexander. *Revolution and Elite Access: Some Hypotheses on Aspects of Political Change.* University of California, Davis: Institute of Governmental Affairs, 1966.

Gurr, Ted Robert. "A Causal Model of Civil Strife: A Comparative Analysis Using New Indices." *American Political Science Review,* 62 (December 1968), pp. 1104–24.

——. "Psychological Factors in Civil Violence." *World Politics,* 20 (January 1968), pp. 245–78.

——. "Sources of Rebellion in Western Societies: Some Quantitative Evidence." *The Annals,* 391 (September 1970), pp. 128–44.

——. "Urban Disorders: Perspectives from the Comparative Study of Civil Strife." *American Behavioral Scientist,* 10 (March–April 1968), pp. 50–55.

——. *Why Men Rebel.* Princeton, N.J.: Princeton University Press, 1970.

—— with Charles Ruttenberg. *The Conditions of Civil Violence: First Tests of a Causal Model.* Princeton University: Center of International Studies, 1967.

Halpern, Manfred. "Redefinition of the Revolutionary Situation." *Journal of International Affairs,* 23 (1969), pp. 54–75.

Hatto, Arthur. " 'Revolution': An Inquiry into the Usefulness of an Historical Term." *Mind,* 58 (1949), pp. 495–517.

Hoffer, Eric. *The True Believer: Thoughts on the Nature of Mass Movements.* New York: New American Library, 1958.

Hopper, Rex D. "The Revolutionary Process: A Frame of Reference for the Study of Revolutionary Movements." *Social Forces,* 28 (1950), pp. 270–79.

Huntington, Samuel P. *Political Order in Changing Societies.* New Haven, Conn.: Yale University Press, 1968.

———, ed. *Changing Patterns of Military Politics.* New York: Free Press, 1962.

Iglitzin, Lynne B. *Violent Conflict in American Society.* San Francisco: Chandler Publishing Co., 1972.

Johnson, Chalmers. *Revolution and the Social System.* Stanford University: Hoover Institution on War, Revolution, and Peace, 1964.

———. *Revolutionary Change.* Boston: Little, Brown & Co., 1966.

Kautsky, John H. "Revolutionary and Managerial Elites in Modernizing Regimes." *Comparative Politics,* 1 (July 1969), pp. 441–67.

Kelly, George A. and Linda B. Miller. *Internal War and International Systems: Perspectives on Method.* Harvard University: Center for International Affairs, 1969.

Kirchheimer, Otto. "Confining Conditions and Revolutionary Breakthroughs." *American Political Science Review,* 59 (December 1965), pp. 964–74.

Laqueur, Walter. "Revolution." *International Encyclopedia of the Social Sciences.* New York: Macmillan Co. and Free Press, 1968.

Lasswell, Harold D. and Daniel Lerner, eds. *World Revolutionary Elites.* Cambridge, Mass.: M.I.T. Press, 1965.

Le Bon, Gustave. *The Psychology of Revolution.* New York: G. P. Putnam's Sons, 1913.

Lee, Ming T. "The Founders of the Chinese Communist Party: A Study in Revolutionaries." *Civilizations.* 13 (1968), pp. 113–27.

Leiden, Carl and Karl M. Schmitt. *The Politics of Violence: Revolution in the Modern World.* Englewood Cliffs, N.J.: Prentice-Hall, Inc., 1968.

Leites, Nathan and Charles Wolf, Jr. *Rebellion and Authority: An Analytic Essay on Insurgent Conflicts.* Chicago: Markham Publishing Co., 1970.

Lenin, V. I. *"Left-Wing" Communism: An Infantile Disorder* (1920). New York: International Publishers, 1940.

———. *What Is to Be Done?* (1902). New York: International Publishers, 1929.

Liddell Hart, B. H. *Strategy,* revised edition. New York: Frederick A. Praeger, 1954.

Luttwak, Edward. *Coup d'Etat: A Practical Handbook.* New York: Fawcett Books, 1969.

MacIver, Robert M. *The Web of Government,* revised edition. New York: Free Press, 1965.

Mack, Raymond W. and Richard C. Snyder. "The Analysis of Social Conflict: Toward an Overview and Synthesis." *Journal of Conflict Resolution,* (1957), pp. 212–48.

Marcuse, Herbert. *An Essay on Liberation.* Boston: Beacon Press, 1969.

——. *One Dimensional Man.* Boston: Beacon Press, 1964.

McColl, Robert W. "A Political Geography of Revolution: China, Vietnam, and Thailand." *Journal of Conflict Resolution.* 11 (1967), pp. 153–67.

Moore, Barrington, Jr. *The Social Origins of Dictatorship and Democracy.* Boston: Beacon Press, 1967.

Meusel, Alfred. "Revolution and Counter-Revolution." *Encyclopedia of the Social Sciences.* New York: Macmillan Co., 1934.

Neumann, Sigmund. "The International Civil War." *World Politics,* 1 (1949), pp. 333–50.

Nieburg, H. L. *Political Violence: The Behavioral Process.* New York: St. Martin's Press, 1969.

——. "The Threat of Violence and Social Change." *American Political Science Review,* 56 (December 1962), pp. 865–73.

Oppenheimer, Martin. *The Urban Guerrilla.* Chicago: Quadrangle Books, 1969.

Pettee, George S. *The Process of Revolution.* New York: Harper & Bros., 1938.

Rejai, Mostafa. "Guerrilla Communism: China, North Vietnam, Cuba." In Reo M. Christenson et al. *Ideologies and Modern Politics.* New York: Dodd, Mead & Co., 1971.

Riezler, Kurt. "On the Psychology of the Modern Revolution." *Social Research,* 10 (1943), pp. 320–36.

Rosenau, James N., ed. *International Aspects of Civil Strife.* Princeton, N.J.: Princeton University Press, 1964.

Rubenstein, Richard E. *Rebels in Eden: Mass Political Violence in the United States.* Boston: Little, Brown & Co., 1970.

Rummel, R. J. "Dimensions of Conflict Behavior Within Nations, 1946–59." *Journal of Conflict Resolution,* 10 (1966), pp. 65–73.

——. "Dimensions of Foreign and Domestic Conflict Behavior: A Review of Empirical Findings." In Dean G. Pruitt and Richard C. Snyder, eds. *Theory and Research on the*

Causes of War. Englewood Cliffs, N.J.: Prentice-Hall, Inc., 1969.

Russett, Bruce M. "Inequality and Instability: The Relation of Land Tenure to Politics." *World Politics,* 16 (April 1964), pp. 442–54.

Scalapino, Robert A., ed. *The Communist Revolution in Asia.* Englewood Cliffs, N.J.: Prentice-Hall, Inc., 1965.

Schurmann, Franz. "On Revolutionary Conflict." *Journal of International Affairs,* 23 (1969), pp. 36–53.

Selznick, Philip. *The Organizational Weapon: A Study of Bolshevik Strategy and Tactics.* New York: McGraw-Hill Book Co., 1952.

Short, James F., Jr. and Marvin E. Wolfgang, eds. "Collective Violence." *The Annals,* 391 (September 1970), pp. 1–167.

Skolnick, Jerome H. *The Politics of Protest.* New York: Ballantine Books, 1969.

Sorel, Georges. *Reflections on Violence* (1906). New York: Collier Books, 1961.

Sorokin, Pitirim A. *The Sociology of Revolution.* Philadelphia: J. B. Lippincott Co., 1925.

Stone, Lawrence. "Theories of Revolution." *World Politics,* 18 (January 1966), pp. 159–76.

Tannenbaum, Frank. "On Political Stability." *Political Science Quarterly,* 76 (1960), pp. 161–80.

Tanter, Raymond. "Dimensions of Conflict Behavior Within and Between Nations, 1958–60." *Journal of Conflict Resolution,* 10 (1966), pp. 41–64.

——— and Manus Midlarsky. "A Theory of Revolution." *Journal of Conflict Resolution,* 11 (1967), pp. 264–80.

Tilly, Charles. *The Vendée.* Cambridge, Mass.: Harvard University Press, 1964.

Wada, George and James C. Davies. "Riots and Rioters." *Western Political Quarterly,* 10 (1957), pp. 864–74.

Walter, Eugene Victor. *Terror and Resistance: A Study of Political Violence.* New York: Oxford University Press, 1969.

Willer, David and George K. Zollschan. "Prolegomena to a Theory of Revolutions." In G. K. Zollschan and Walter Hirsch, eds. *Explorations in Social Change.* Boston: Houghton Mifflin Co., 1964.

Wolf, Eric R. *Peasant Wars of the Twentieth Century.* New York: Harper & Row, 1969.

Wolfenstein, E. Victor. *The Revolutionary Personality: Lenin,*

Trotsky, Gandhi. Princeton, N.J.: Princeton University Press, 1967.

Wylie, J. C. *Military Strategy: A General Theory of Power Control.* New Brunswick, N.J.: Rutgers University Press, 1967.

Yoder, Dale. "Current Definitions of Revolution." *American Journal of Sociology,* 32 (1926), pp. 433–41.

BOLIVIA

Alexander, Robert J. *The Bolivian National Revolution.* New Brunswick, N.J.: Rutgers University Press, 1958.

——. "Organized Labor and the Bolivian National Revolution." In Everett M. Kasslow, ed. *National Labor Movements in the Postwar World.* Evanston, Ill.: Northwestern University Press, 1963.

——. *Prophets of Revolution: Profiles of Latin American Leaders.* New York: The Macmillan Co., 1962.

——, ed. *Organized Labor in Latin America.* New York: Free Press, 1965.

Arnade, Charles W. "Communism in Latin America." *South Atlantic Quarterly,* 53 (1954), pp. 454–63.

Blasier, Cole. "Studies of Revolution: Origins in Mexico, Bolivia, and Cuba." *Latin American Research Review,* 2 (Summer 1967), pp. 28–64.

Flores, Edmundo. "Land Reform in Bolivia." *Land Economics,* 30 (May 1954), pp. 112–24.

Foreign Areas Studies Division, Special Operations Research Office, The American University. *U. S. Army Area Handbook for Bolivia.* Washington, D.C.: U. S. Government Printing Office, 1963.

Heath, Dwight B. "Bolivia: Peasant Syndicates Among the Aymara of the Yungas—A View from the Grass Roots." In Henry A. Landsberger, ed. *Latin American Peasant Movements.* Ithaca, N.Y.: Cornell University Press, 1969.

——, Charles J. Erasmus, and Hans C. Buechler. *Land Reform and Social Revolution in Bolivia.* New York: Frederick A. Praeger, 1969.

Herring, Hubert. *A History of Latin America.* New York: Alfred A. Knopf, 1962.

Hinton, Ronald, ed. *Who's Who in Latin America,* 3rd ed., Part IV. Stanford, Calif.: Stanford University Press, 1947.

Klein, Herbert S. "The Crisis of Legitimacy and the Origins of Social Revolution: The Bolivian Experience." *Journal of Inter-American Studies*, 10 (January 1968), pp. 102–16.

——. *Parties and Political Change in Bolivia, 1880–1952.* Cambridge, Eng.: Cambridge University Press, 1969.

Malloy, James M. *Bolivia: The Uncompleted Revolution.* Pittsburgh, Pa.: University of Pittsburgh Press, 1970.

Osborne, Harold. *Bolivia: A Land Divided,* 2nd ed. London: Royal Institute of International Affairs, 1955.

Ostria Gutiérrez, Alberto. *The Tragedy of Bolivia: A People Crucified.* New York: Devin-Adair Co., 1958.

Patch, Richard W. "Bolivia: The Restrained Revolution." *The Annals,* 334 (March 1961), pp. 123–32.

——. "Bolivia: U.S. Assistance in a Revolutionary Setting." In Richard Adams et al. *Social Change in Latin America Today.* New York: Harper & Bros., 1963.

——. "The Bolivian Falange." *AUFS Reports: West Coast South America Series,* Vol. VI. New York: American Universities Field Staff, Inc., 1959.

——. "The Last of Bolivia's MNR?" *AUFS Reports: West Coast South America Series,* Vol. XI. New York: American Universities Field Staff, Inc., 1964.

——. "Peasantry and National Revolution: Bolivia." In K. H. Silvert, ed., *Expectant Peoples: Nationalism and Development.* New York: Random House, 1963.

——. "Personalities and Politics in Bolivia." *AUFS Reports: West Coast South America Series,* Vol. IX. New York: American Universities Field Staff, Inc., 1962.

Stokes, William S. "The 'Revolución Nacional' and the MNR in Bolivia." *Inter-American Economic Affairs,* 12 (Spring 1959), pp. 28–53.

U. S. Department of State. *The Chaco Peace Conference.* Washington, D.C.: U. S. Government Printing Office, 1940.

Weston, Charles H. "An Ideology of Modernization: The Case of the Bolivian MNR." *Journal of Inter-American Studies,* 10 (January 1968), pp. 85–101.

Whitaker, Arthur P. *The United States and South America: The Northern Republics.* Cambridge, Mass.: Harvard University Press, 1948.

Zondag, Cornelius H. *The Bolivian Economy, 1952–65: The Revolution and Its Aftermath.* New York: Frederick A. Praeger, 1966.

NORTH VIETNAM

Buttinger, Joseph. *Vietnam: A Political History*. New York: Frederick A. Praeger, 1968.

Cady, John F. *Southeast Asia: Its Historical Development*. New York: McGraw-Hill Book Co., 1964.

Duncanson, Dennis J. *Government and Revolution in Vietnam*. London: Oxford University Press, 1968.

Elliott-Batesman, Michael. *Defeat in the East: The Mark of Mao Tse-tung on War*. London: Oxford University Press, 1967.

Fall, Bernard B. *Hell in a Very Small Place: The Siege of Dien Bien Phu*. New York: Vintage Books, 1968.

——. *Street Without Joy: Insurgency in Indochina, 1946–63*, 3rd rev. ed. Harrisburg, Pa.: Stackpole Co., 1963.

——. *The Two Vietnams: A Political and Military Analysis*, 2nd ed. New York: Frederick A. Praeger, 1967.

——. *The Vietminh Regime*. New York: Institute of Pacific Relations, 1956.

——, ed. *Ho Chi Minh on Revolution*. New York: Signet Books, 1968.

Giap, Vo Nguyên. *People's War, People's Army*. New York: Bantam Books, 1968.

Hoang Van Chi. *From Colonialism to Communism: A Case History of North Vietnam*. New York: Frederick A. Praeger, 1964.

Honey, J. P. *Communism in North Vietnam*. Cambridge, Mass.: M.I.T. Press, 1963.

Johnson, Chalmers. "The Third Generation of Guerrilla Warfare." *Asian Survey*, 8 (June 1968), pp. 435–47.

Lacouture, Jean. *Ho Chi Minh: A Political Biography*. New York: Random House, 1968.

——. *Vietnam: Between Two Truces*. New York: Random House, 1968.

McAlister, John T., Jr. *Viet Nam: The Origins of Revolution*. New York: Alfred A. Knopf, 1969.

Modelski, George. "The Viet Minh Complex." In Cyril E. Black, ed. *Communism and Revolution: The Strategic Uses of Political Violence*. Princeton, N.J.: Princeton University Press, 1964.

O'Ballance, Edgar. *The Indo-China War, 1945–1954: A Study in Guerrilla Warfare*. London: Faber & Faber, 1964.

Pike, Douglas. *Viet Cong: The Organization and Techniques of the National Liberation Front of South Vietnam*. Cambridge, Mass.: M.I.T. Press, 1966.

Sacks, I. Milton. "Marxism in Viet Nam." In Frank N. Trager, ed. *Marxism in Southeast Asia*. Stanford, Calif.: Stanford University Press, 1959.

Tanham, George K. *Communist Revolutionary Warfare: From the Vietminh to the Viet Cong*, rev. ed. New York: Frederick A. Praeger, 1967.

FRANCE

Ardagh, John. *The New French Revolution*. New York: Harper & Row, 1969.

Aron, Raymond. *The Elusive Revolution: Anatomy of a Student Revolt*. New York: Frederick A. Praeger, 1969.

Birnbaum, Norman. *The Crisis of Industrial Society*. New York: Oxford University Press, 1969.

Bourges, Hervé, ed. *The French Student Revolt: The Leaders Speak*. New York: Hill & Wang, 1968.

Brown, Bernard E. *The French Revolt: May 1968*. New York: McCaleb-Seiler Publishing Co., 1970.

Cohn-Bendit, Daniel and Gabriel Cohn-Bendit. *Obsolete Communism: The Left-Wing Alternative*. New York: McGraw-Hill, 1968.

Ehrenreich, Barbara and John Ehrenreich. *Long March, Short Spring: The Student Uprising at Home and Abroad*. New York: Monthly Review Press, 1969.

Lefebvre, Henri. *The Explosion: Marxism and the French Revolution*. New York: Monthly Review Press, 1969.

Lichtheim, George. "What Happened in France," *Commentary*, 46 (September 1968), pp. 39–49.

Mendel, Arthur P. "Why the French Communists Stopped the Revolution." *Review of Politics*, 31 (January 1969), pp. 3–27.

Posner, Charles, ed. *Reflections on the Revolution in France: 1968*. Baltimore: Penguin Books, 1970.

Priaulx, Allan and Sanford J. Unger. *The Almost Revolution, France—1968*. New York: Dell Publishing Co., 1969.

Quattrocchi, Angelo and Tom Nairn. *The Beginning of the End: France, May 1968*. London: Panther Books, Ltd., 1968.

Seale, Patrick and Maureen McConville, *Red Flag/Black Flag: French Revolution, 1968.* New York: Ballantine Books, 1968.

Servan-Schreiber, J. J. *The Spirit of May.* New York: McGraw-Hill Book Co., 1969.

Taylor, Edmond. "Revolution and Reaction in France." *Foreign Affairs,* 47 (October 1968), pp. 99–109.

Waterman, Harvey. *Political Change in Contemporary France: The Politics of an Industrial Democracy.* Columbus, Ohio: Charles E. Merrill, 1969.

Wilson, Frank L. "The French Left and the Elections of 1968." *World Politics,* 21 (July 1969), pp. 539–74.

INDEX